What people a  T0168501

Expanding Scriptures: Lost and Found

Don MacGregor's little book, *Expanding Scriptures: Lost and Found*, is a beauty. In a compact way, he covers an accurate history of the Bible, a wise and helpful understanding of biblical interpretation, a comprehensive look at "lost" gospels, and a well-researched understanding of the Bible for today's world. Highly recommended for personal study and group discussion.
Revd. Paul Smith, co-founder of the Integral Christian Network, and author of *Integral Christianity: The Spirit's Call to Evolve* and *Is Your God Big Enough? Close Enough? You Enough? Jesus and the Three Faces of God*

By exploring Christianity as a path of personal transformation rather than a transactional relationship with the divine and a reward of salvation, *Expanding Scriptures: Lost and Found* accomplishes a wonderful and extremely timely service to spiritual seekers, whether Christian or otherwise. Its invitation, to live questions of the deeper meaning of life as way-showers leading eventually to the unfolding of answers, is the basis of all perennial wisdom teachings. Whilst the paths are myriad, as this profoundly insightful book shows, the destination is constant; the discerning and eventual experience of unity and oneness as the true state of the world's and our meaning and existence.
Dr Jude Currivan. Cosmologist, author of *The Cosmic Hologram* and co-founder WholeWorld-View, www.wholeworld-view.org

Expanding Scriptures: Lost and Found is packed with direct, realistic spiritual wisdom, much needed for our modern world. Don MacGregor's words shine a bright light through the dark confusion of outdated thinking. This is cutting edge theology and a brilliant introduction to Biblical history, including the lost gospels of the New Testament, the real Jesus and Mary Magdalene. Every Christian minister and Bible Study Group should read it. I promise the journey will be one of transformation and enlightenment.

Pam Evans MBE, Founder of the multi award winning Peace Mala educational charity for Global Citizenship and World Peace, and author of *Sharing the Light: Walking for World Peace with the Celtic Saints of Gower* and *How the Wisdom of the Ages is Reflected in Many World Faiths*

As Christianity loses its ground and finds itself in a crisis, a return to the original message of Christ becomes an existential need for its future evolution. Don MacGregor has done a wonderful work by pointing out this essential truth in his second book of "The Wisdom Series" *Exploring Scriptures: Lost and Found*. I recommend this book to all those who seek the original, universal and transforming message of Christ. I am sure it will satisfy their intellectual quest and longing of the heart.

Br. John Martin Sahajananda, spiritual director of the Shantivanam Ashram in India, author of *You Are The Light, Hindu Christ, The Four O'Clock Talks, Mission Without Conversion* and others

Wisdom is a gift of ages past, but also a resource forever inviting us into expanded horizons of meaning. Don MacGregor situates his exploration of Christian scripture between these two strands. While honouring the past his goal is to facilitate movement into the expanding horizons of faith that engage us today. A valuable and useful guide for spiritual seekers of our time.

Fr. Diarmuid O'Murchu, author of *Quantum Theology: Spiritual Implications of the New Physics* and *Incarnation: A New Evolutionary Threshold* plus many others

I recommend *Expanding Scriptures: Lost and Found* to anyone who is ready to consider and understand the next step in the evolution of Christian thought and the expansion of human consciousness. The book explores the true origins of the New Testament, and includes an enriching overview of some of the lost codices of early Christianity. Dedicated to the idea that religious thought must evolve to meet the times, the author weaves together the Christian teachings with the truths found within science, psychology and the Perennial Philosophy.

William Meader, International speaker and author of *Shine Forth: The Soul's Magical Destiny*, Portland, Oregon, USA

Don MacGregor offers a profound and practical understanding of the history and essence of the Bible as relevant and related to the Ageless Wisdom at the heart of all the world's religions. *Expanding Scriptures: Lost and Found* is a timely presentation and provides a sacred, informative and reflective journey for all those seeking to realize the beauty of the differentiation of Truth from one source, one unity of purpose, and grasp the meaning of the language within Christianity. We are held in the Divine Presence; it flows through everything; and our recognition of the depth and breadth of our interconnectedness with all Life, and with Mother Nature ushers us into a New Day, one that yields right relationship throughout the manifest world. We are offered the opportunity to question, reflect and realize that our worldview is shifting once again and it is the essence of life that is perennial. This is a book you will be glad you opened!

Dr. Dot Maver, educator and peacebuilder, founder of Global Silent Minute and co-author of *Conscious Education: The Bridge to Freedom*

This is a fascinating and brilliant book for anyone who wants to acquaint themselves with the transformational teachings that Jesus really taught and which we learn about in the recently discovered Nag Hammadi gospels (especially in the Gospels of Thomas and of Mary). Don reminds us that the bible needs to be seen through fresh eyes. It must not be interpreted literally, as it is a selection of different genres written by many different people for different reasons, over centuries. Consequently it is a product of the worldview or cultures of those differing times, and needs reinterpreting in the complex world which we face in 2021. He reveals how outmoded our current theology is, steeped as it is in violent tribalism and patriarchy. He shows how the real and deep mystical, esoteric teachings can be found in the recently discovered Nag Hammadi texts, especially the Gospel of Thomas, where Jesus talks much more like a Zen Master or Master Shaman. After every chapter, Don gives us further resources and important questions to ask ourselves. This important book is an absolute must read for all Christians interested in asking themselves new questions about their religion and who are truly committed to using Christianity as a direct path to God.

Dr. Serge Beddington-Behrens, PhD. Psychotherapist, Spiritual Guide and author of *Gateways to the Soul* and *Awakening the Universal Heart*

Expanding Scriptures Lost and Found

THE WISDOM SERIES BOOK 2

Expanding Scriptures Lost and Found

THE WISDOM SERIES BOOK 2

Don MacGregor

CHRISTIAN ALTERNATIVE
BOOKS

Winchester, UK
Washington, USA

JOHN HUNT PUBLISHING

First published by Christian Alternative Books, 2021
Christian Alternative Books is an imprint of John Hunt Publishing Ltd.,
No. 3 East St., Alresford, Hampshire SO24 9EE, UK
office@jhpbooks.com
www.johnhuntpublishing.com
www.christian-alternative.com

For distributor details and how to order please visit the 'Ordering' section on our website.

Text copyright: Don MacGregor 2020

ISBN: 978 1 78904 866 7
978 1 78904 867 4 (ebook)
Library of Congress Control Number: 2020951034

A CIP catalogue record for this book is available from the British Library.

Design: Stuart Davies

UK: Printed and bound by CPI Group (UK) Ltd, Croydon, CR0 4YY
Printed in North America by CPI GPS partners

We operate a distinctive and ethical publishing philosophy in
all areas of our business, from our global network of authors to
production and worldwide distribution.

Contents

Previous Titles by the author

Blue Sky God: The Evolution of Science and Christianity.
Circle Books, John Hunt Publishing, 2012
ISBN 978-1-84694-937-1

Christianity Expanding: Into Universal Spirituality.
The Wisdom Series Book 1. Christian Alternative Books,
John Hunt Publishing, 2020
ISBN 978-1-78904-422-5

Introduction

This is the second book in "The Wisdom Series" the aim of which is twofold, firstly to recognise that Christianity is a path of transformation as taught by Jesus, and was never meant to be a transaction between the individual and a distant God, in order to be "saved". The path of transformation is there in the Bible and Christian theology as we know it, but is not the main emphasis of Church teachings. It is also there in many of the "lost Christianities" that were ruled out as the church gained in power and control. These alternative scriptures are now coming to the fore as a result of rediscoveries in the last seventy years or so, challenging mainstream theological viewpoints.

The second aim is to link this path of transformation with the Esoteric Philosophy or Perennial Wisdom teachings, thus giving a suitable and more expansive framework for Christianity in the twenty-first century. This philosophy really sees the spiritual path in terms of consciousness and energy, containing many different levels of being which overlap with each other. A key point is that each human being is made up of a personality and a Soul. The personality has a mental, an emotional and a physical nature, all of which keep us grounded in this physical reality of space and time – and so we live out a single life with all its struggles and suffering, its pain and heartache, and its joys and delights. This life is also a "vale of soul-making", an idea developed by both Origen and Irenaeus, early Christian theologians.

Esoteric philosophy takes it further, seeing the Soul as the eternal aspect of the human being, our true nature. The evolving Soul undertakes successive incarnations as it gradually attains higher levels of consciousness, until the stage of a "Soul-filled personality" is reached. This is the stage in which the personality has relinquished its self-centred control and has allowed the eternal Soul to be fully expressed in the world. Thus the path of transformation is extended into a much greater sphere of being, a much longer path than just the one short life in which we pass or fail to end up in heaven or hell.

The existing theology of Christianity in the West contains the idea of sanctification, being "made holy", which is fine as far as it goes – but it does not go far enough to my mind. It falls short when we ask what happens to those who are not "sanctified" by the time they die, whereas the bigger framework of many lives gives opportunity for further evolution of consciousness, and sanctification over a much larger timescale. This evolution in consciousness is something which happens not just to individuals, but to the human race as a whole in its progression through the ages.

How we understand scriptures is an important part of this journey, which is the focus of this short book. We shall cover how the Bible came about, what was once lost but is now found and should be included (particularly a more central role for the Gospel of Thomas and Mary Magdalene), how interpretations vary and why, what reinterpretations can be helpful, and the strangeness and importance of numerology.

Book 2 is designed to be suitable for both study groups and individuals and each chapter has questions for reflection and further resources to follow up.

Chapter 1

The Bible and How It Came About

Why just the Bible?

Firstly, an important question: why am I only considering the Christian Scriptures in this book? There are so many other enlightening, inspired and wise texts within other religious traditions, so why not look at them? I have no wish to detract from them at all, but my reasoning is that much has already been written about those sources of wisdom, whereas relatively little has been written on enlarging the Christian scriptures with the texts in the *lost and found* category. I think there is another way of looking at the transformative message within the Bible, which means that we have to also look at the other texts that were around in the early days of Christianity, about which most Christians, on the whole, know very little, even though they have been around for many decades.

My view of the Bible is that it is a starting point, not an end point. It is a launch pad, not an end destination. It can help sustain us and inspire us on the journey of life, but to treat it as a final revelation, a spiritual terminus, is to restrict and close down the journey of divine revelation, limiting our understanding to that of the writer of the text. Hence, I have a great respect for rich scriptures from other traditions, and from more contemporary writings, seeing new and alternative insights through those lenses. But here in this book, I am concentrating on the Christian and Hebrew Scriptures we have inherited in the Bible – and also those Christian texts that didn't make the cut, the other versions that were excluded for one reason or another, but have now resurfaced. We now know much more about the early diversity of Christianity from them.

The Book of Books

I remember the first time I had to stand up and give the Bible reading in Church. I was thirty-three years old, had been teaching in a secondary school for seven years, with classes of thirty, and speaking to assemblies of about four hundred students. But when, as a fairly new Christian convert, I stood up at the church lectern to read a passage from the Bible, printed in front of me to read, my legs were trembling with nerves! Why? It was something to do with the responsibility of it – this was the *Word of God*, to be read out loud, reverently – and faultlessly. At least, that was my conditioning at the time! It had to do with the idea that the Bible was one complete revelation, virtually dictated by God, the all-time truth. I soon began to question that and look deeper into how it came about.

We often refer to the Bible as the "book of books", and so it is, probably the most influential collection of literature in the world's history. It still hits the top spot in the best-sellers. But it is also quite literally a book of books – the Old Testament, now referred to as the Hebrew Scriptures, containing thirty-nine of them, and the New Testament twenty-seven, making sixty-six altogether. We can tend to forget that it is a selection of all sorts of different genres from different times, and needs to be treated as such. The Greek word from which we derive our word Bible is *ta biblia*, literally "the books". They were written over a very long period of time – scholars think that the earliest composition in the Old Testament is the Song of Deborah in Judges 5. It may date from 1100 BCE, that is, two or three centuries earlier than the Greek writer Homer (if he actually existed! Many scholars think not). The latest in the Hebrew Scriptures is the book of Daniel from the second century BCE, making a total span of 1000 years. (For "The Old Testament in a Nutshell", see Appendix.)

When we add in the books of the New Testament, which are nearly all written in the first Christian century, we extend this period to as much as twelve hundred years. Think how we have changed in that length of time! It would take us from about 800 CE amidst a feudal society, the time of the Viking invasions and the Danelaw, right up to the present day and the proliferation of the written word everywhere. That period takes us through all sorts of different human experience and cultures, a variety of ways of looking at and understanding the world – and an evolution in human consciousness. Any writings from the different periods in that one thousand two hundred-year span have to be understood within their time, context and culture. Similarly, we cannot expect to treat all the content of the Bible in the same way. In terms of content, they range from tribal history to mythical and historical stories, to poetry and visions, to personal letters. Beside the range of content, there is the issue of social change. We change; our understanding of society and the world around us changes, our level of awakened consciousness changes. If we remember that just five hundred years ago it was accepted by society that you could be beheaded or burnt at the stake for having the wrong religious belief, we can see how much we have changed in that time. It is the evolution of consciousness.

However, deep mystical wisdom pre-dates and transcends time and contains truths that resonate down through the age. They are timeless. So in all main religious traditions we find a form of the *Golden Rule*, "Do to others as you would have them do to you." In all traditions, we find humanity has spiritual experiences, as if there is a divine seed within each of us waiting to burst out of its shell if we provide the right conditions for growth. Those experiences become "encultured" in their own language of the time. In all ages there is an intermingling of ideas, where one belief influences another.

During the Babylonian captivity, the writers of the first five books of the Hebrew Scriptures, called the "Deuteronomists", were strongly influenced by Zoroastrianism, one of the world's oldest continuously practised religions. They wrote their account and understanding of God to remind the captive peoples of their past, before it faded from memories. Historical features of Zoroastrianism, such as ideas of a messiah, judgement after death, heaven and hell, and free will crept in and influenced the writers of these early scriptures. During New Testament times, Greek philosophy had a strong influence on the development of theological thinking. The Platonic Theory of Forms had an enormous influence on Christian views of God in the Greek-speaking world. In those philosophies, "forms" were the ideals of every object in the physical world, and objects in the physical world were merely shadows of those perfect forms, like patterns at a higher level. This is an expression of the Esoteric Philosophy, that there are other planes of being, which are more "real" than this physical one. This type of interplay between philosophies was and is still very common. No religion is an island.

How did we arrive at the New Testament?

We refer to the New Testament collection of writing as the Christian *canon*, a Greek word meaning "list", in this case a list of books authorised by the church. But that authorisation did not happen until well over *three hundred years* after Jesus' time. It is a story of power and control and the adoption of Christianity by the Roman Empire.

There were many other variant scriptures circulating before that which gave many different interpretations of Christianity. These show other viable versions of Christianity, using these scriptures as their basis. What happened to them is a tale of winners and losers in the evolution of Christian theology. What we have inherited is the winners' version. How was this winners' version of the New Testament decided upon? It emerged slowly, influenced by various writers who were beginning to work out what their favourite texts were. Initially, Christianity was just a sect within Judaism, and some writers, such as Bishop John Spong, believe that the gospels of Mark and Matthew were written to fit in with the Festival and Sabbath readings in the synagogue. In his theory, the traditional Hebrew Scripture readings were followed by a passage from Mark (for the major festivals), or Matthew (for the ordinary Sabbath readings). (See John Spong, *Liberating the Gospels*.)

The New Testament as a defined whole did not exist for the first three to four hundred years after Jesus died. That often comes as a surprise to many churchgoers. There were many different groups of Christians who formed their own communities and followed their own selection of writings, or simply the ones that they could get hold of as books were in limited supply in those pre-printing days. As time went on into the third and fourth centuries, certain favourites appeared and there were heated discussions and exchanges about what were the best texts to use. The letters of Paul were some of the earliest – the letters to the Galatians and Corinthians may have been written in the early 50s CE. But scholars say about half the letters that are claimed to be written by Paul were probably written later by his followers in the style of Paul – which was an accepted practice back then. It might be seen as fake news now! They work out by grammatical and linguistic style and content whether they think it is a genuine Pauline letter, or written by one of his followers.

The first list to appear was written by Marcion of Sinope around the middle of the second century. He declared that everything that was not on his list was "in error". That list had ten letters attributed to Paul and only parts, not all, of the gospel of Luke. No other gospels at all! His theology was quite radical and Church Fathers such as Justin Martyr, Irenaeus, and Tertullian denounced him as a heretic, and he was excommunicated by the church of Rome around 144 CE. Most of his writings were burnt. Irenaeus was probably the first person to designate Matthew, Mark, Luke and John as the most authoritative gospels, but his justification for that was rather strange by today's reasoning. He said one must have four gospels since there are four corners to the earth and the wind blows from four directions!

As an aside, please remember that no one actually knows who wrote the four gospels. Most scholars today recognize that the books were written by otherwise unknown but relatively well-educated Greek-speaking (and writing) Christians during the second half of the first century. They weren't called the gospels of Matthew, Mark, Luke and John until the latter half of the second century, one hundred years later. Writing around 150–160 CE, Justin Martyr quotes verses from them, but simply terms them the "Memoires of the Apostles." It was not until 180–185 that Irenaeus started to credit them to the apostles.

From 190–310 CE there seems to have been little interest in forming an authoritative list of scriptures for the Christian communities, probably because they were defending themselves from various criticisms from without, followed by a number of persecutions, so internal arguments were on hold. Even the famous Council of Nicaea in 325 CE didn't produce a list of the authorised books in the New Testament. It was more concerned with defining in great detail who Jesus was. A decisive moment is documented in 367 CE when Athanasius, the theologian Bishop of Alexandria, wrote a "festal letter" at Easter, instructing the Christians of North Africa to use only a certain twenty-seven books as authoritative texts.

Athanasius was a charismatic, powerful man, but had a stormy time and was excommunicated at one stage, then reinstated, then deposed as bishop in the midst of the Arian controversy over the status of Father, Son and Holy Spirit. Athanasius battled through his intermittent episcopacy which spanned forty-five years (328–373 CE). Seventeen of those years were spent in five exiles, when he was replaced on the order of four different Roman emperors. He was hardly one of the winners during his lifetime. A theological battle had been raging for about fifty years since the Nicene Creed was formed, along with political struggles and many changes of Roman emperor, which all contributed to the mix. His Latin nickname was apparently *Athanasius Contra Mundum* or *Athanasius Against the World*! But he was an influential figure, and his choice of books to be read carried a lot of weight.

However, even in the fifth and sixth centuries, the canon was still not firmly fixed. The Revelation of John was often dropped and other texts such as the "Shepherd of Hermas" and "Letters from Clement" were included. But in Western Christianity, from the seventh century onwards, the accepted New Testament as we know it now was used. It is what survived the years of debate and argument and opinion. It was all influenced by politics, power and control as the various bishops and emperors vied with each other for influence. If we could start again now and rationally assess all the different texts available, I am sure there would be some other inclusions, and probably some considerable deletions, but the weight of tradition makes change very difficult. Some scholars have had a go at this, notably the Fellows of the Jesus Seminar, a large group of biblical scholars founded in 1985 by Robert Funk.

What I really want to look at is what was lost, but has been rediscovered, because some of those lost scriptures contain other versions, maybe truer versions, of Jesus' teaching! These alternative scriptures will be addressed in Chapter 2 onwards.

An Evolution in Understanding

The Bible overall is a record of Jewish and surviving early Christian experience of their understanding of God. But it is always based on someone's *experience and understanding*. It was written by fallible people, probably all male, who trusted in God and interpreted their life experience through that lens and hence felt that they were guided by God. In the stories of the Hebrew people we see an initial belief that *their* God is the hope and promise of Israel. Their God was in competition with the gods of other tribes, such as Baal, Marduk and Dagon. In their written history, we can see a hesitant unfoldment of the universal nature of God. They gradually moved from thinking that God was their own tribal deity, the God for their nation, to a higher understanding that there is only one God, one Divine Being, one Source. The writers were human beings trying to express their inspiration and understanding within their own time and culture. To gain the most from them, we have to reinterpret their writings for today, not just take them at literal face value.

Even though they came to an understanding that there is only one God, they were still stuck in a tribal mentality that said this one God could only be worshipped correctly in one particular way – and that was carried through into Christianity. This is the root cause of religious wars, believing that God only likes religious rituals to happen in one particular way. If God were able to laugh, that's probably a good joke for him/her, if it were not for the trouble it has caused in arguments, divisions and strife. The prophet Isaiah saw through the meaningless rituals of the Hebrews and spoke in no uncertain terms.

What to me is the multitude of your sacrifices? says the LORD; I have had enough of burnt offerings of rams and the fat of fed beasts; I do not delight in the blood of bulls, or of lambs, or of goats. When you come to appear before me, who asked this from your hand? Trample my courts no more; bringing offerings is futile; incense is an abomination to me. New moon and Sabbath and calling of convocation—I cannot endure solemn assemblies with iniquity. Your new moons and your appointed festivals my soul hates; they have become a burden to me, I am weary of bearing them. (Isaiah 1:11–14)

Isaiah's call from God was for the people to renew their inner attitudes, to move to a higher way of thinking, to change the way they behaved, not just perform a ritualistic act to make everything right:

Wash yourselves; make yourselves clean; remove the evil of your doings from before my eyes; cease to do evil, learn to do good; seek justice, rescue the oppressed, defend the orphan, plead for the widow. (Isaiah 1:16–17)

We find the same call to inner compassion and right living from Micah:

"With what shall I come before the LORD, and bow myself before God on high? Shall I come before him with burnt offerings, with calves a year old? Will the LORD be pleased with thousands of rams, with ten thousands of rivers of oil? Shall I give my firstborn for my transgression, the fruit of my body for the sin of my soul?" He has told you, O mortal, what is good; and what does the LORD require of you but to do justice, and to love kindness, and to walk humbly with your God? (Micah 6:6–8)

This is saying that the rituals are not the path to transformation, they are an outer form to aid inner change. If the inner change is not happening, the outer form is futile and useless. The Bible is part of the outer form, there to encourage inner change as we walk the path to enlightenment. Just because someone goes to church, sings hymns and receives Holy Communion, it does not make them a Christian if there has been no inner transformative change. This is the message of Esoteric Philosophy, that we are all on a path of evolution of consciousness, moving from lower, coarser vibrational levels of spiritual energy to higher, finer ones.

Biblical Criticism

When I entered into Christianity, the door I went through was of an evangelical, charismatic church, which was right for me at the time, and the idea that you could "criticise" the Bible was radical. But in the last one hundred years or so, scholars have applied themselves to examining the Bible in many new ways, not just taking it literally. This is very much in line with the way early scholars understood it, such as Origen (185-253 CE), looking for metaphorical understandings that access underlying messages. These different critical ways of looking at the text of the Bible have asked a series of different questions, such as:

- Is the text we have a faithful rendering of the original?
- What were the sources that might have been used by the author?
- What was the historical and cultural context of the author?
- Is there any evidence that the author is really the one traditionally assigned?
- What genre of literature is the writing?
- What accepted literary norms from then are not understood now?
- What was the intention of the author and who was he addressing?
- What did the text say to the original reader, and what does it say now?
- Can we take this text literally or is it analogy and myth with a deeper meaning?

This digs deep into the texts and brings up different ways of interpreting, often challenging previous theologies, such as the views about slavery, women and homosexuality. It is vital that we allow changing attitudes and social mores to challenge our Christian theology, which was formed in previous times. Unfortunately, much of that important work has stayed in the preserve of academia and has not percolated down to grass roots level in the churches and church theology. The result is that we have inherited a theology formed hundreds of years ago with concepts that have been long superseded by discoveries in physics, chemistry, biology, astronomy, psychology, archaeology, sociology and almost any other "ology" you can think of. Small wonder that it is sidelined by most younger generations today. One of the biggest problems is the way in which theology is enshrined in liturgy and hymns, and some of the hymns can be quite unpalatable to people today.

Best and Worst

The Bible could be called both the best book in the world and the worst book in the world, because its use depends on human behaviour, which is both exalted and debased. How we use the Bible depends on our own level of enlightenment. The scriptures are seen at their worst when they are used for controlling, threatening and self-gratifying behaviour, the expression of the lower, self-centred mind. They are at their best when they are used for the healing of the world and for the transformation of the self, informed by the Soul. It all depends on how we read them and how we use them. *Who* we are will determine *how* we understand the Bible and *how* we use it. The individual authors of the different books had their own life experience, their own culture and their own personalities, and all that was involved in their writing. Some of that writing is what we call "inspired", in that those who wrote were seeking to access a level beyond, a finer vibrational understanding. They touched in to intuition from soul level coming from beyond this physical realm, and then expressed it in their own terms. However, because this expression happens using the language and stage of evolution of their own culture, some of it is comes over today as retrograde, demeaning and coming from a totally different understanding of the world. Some of it has been written with a three steps forward progressive viewpoint, and some with a two steps backward, regressive view. Our task is to discern which is which! When I was a curate, my rector was of the opinion that about half the Hebrew Scriptures should be deleted from the Bible! Yet within all the mix, there are gems to be found, such as the instruction to "Choose Life!" in Deuteronomy 30:19, and to "love your neighbour as yourself" in Leviticus 19:18.

The Bible is not an answer book, so that we can somehow "know" God as an intellectual exercise. It is only in walking the journey of faith, hope, and love itself that we come to know the real answers. Biblical answers are not usually direct answers in guidance for life. They are hardly ever "head" answers. They are most often "heart", "gut" and "soul" answers and need careful discernment. In fact, answers that come too quickly often need to be waited on and deliberated on to get to the depth of them. It's why Jesus used parables – so that people had to work it out for themselves, chew it over, work it through. The poet Rainer Marie Rilke put it like this.

Have patience with everything unresolved in your heart
and try to love the questions themselves...
Don't search for the answers
which could not be given you now,
because you would not be able to live them.
And the point is, to live everything.
Live the questions now.
Perhaps then, someday in the future,
you will gradually, without even noticing it,
live your way into the answer.

The First Bible and Ecological Awareness

Some spiritual greats, such as Anthony of the Desert and Thomas Aquinas, have said that the first Bible is creation, the divine revelation spoken out into materiality. The first Bible started to be "written" at least 13.7 billion years ago, at the moment that we call the Big Bang. St Paul said, "Ever since God created the world, God's everlasting power and divinity—however invisible—are there for the mind to see in the things that God has made" (Romans 1:20). Maybe if the Church had emphasised that more, we would have had more respect for the world around us, a more ecological faith. We now find ourselves in the situation of a looming climate crisis and many look to the indigenous faiths and beliefs to find a more harmonious way of living. To quote an old saying, we became "so spiritually minded as to be no earthly use", in terms of caring for creation.

Many people have had deep spiritual experiences through immersion in nature. Belief in God for me has been reinforced through experiencing the presence of God in the quiet moments when heaven breaks through into this earthly reality. I've definitely felt that at times. I remember one time back in the 1990s, living in Leicester, UK, when I drove up to the Derbyshire Peak District for an overnight camp and a day's walking. It was mid July, and I got up early the next morning and strode out of Edale village and up the path leading to the top of Kinderscout, which is a plateau about two thousand feet above sea level. It is covered in deep peat, into which water has carved huge ravines all over, in places exposing the underlying white limestone. It was a beautiful, still, sunny morning, and no one had been ahead of me or had followed me, so I knew I was the only one up there.

As I walked across, up and down these peat ravines, I suddenly became aware that the only thing I could hear was my own breathing and heartbeat. It had been dry for weeks, making the peat form huge springy cushions, and my footsteps were totally muffled. There were no bird calls around. Walking silently on this soft, black peat, interspersed with outcrops of white limestone sparkling in the sun, I was conscious of something beyond what I could see, a unity that was holding it all in being. There was a presence in the silence that was in me, in the air, in the peat, in the rock. There was an interconnectedness about it all, a oneness that said we were all held in God. I can't explain it, I can't detail some majestic vision, but I know I felt it. It was real to me, unseen but real. St Paul said something about this in his letter to the Corinthians.

Even though our outer nature is wasting away, our inner nature is being renewed day by day. For this slight momentary affliction [i.e. this life] is preparing us for an eternal weight of glory beyond all measure, because we look not at what can be seen but at what cannot be seen; for what can be seen is temporary, but what cannot be seen is eternal. (2 Corinthians 4:16–18)

After telling of this experience to my spiritual director, he sent me this poem, "The Moor" by R. S. Thomas:

The Moor
It was like a church to me.
I entered it on soft foot,
Breath held like a cap in the hand.
It was quiet.
What God was there made himself felt,
Not listened to, in clean colours
That brought a moistening of the eye,
In movement of the wind over grass
There were no prayers said.
But the stillness of the heart's passions;
That was praise enough;
And the mind's cession
Of its kingdom. I walked on,
Simple and poor, while the air crumbled
And broke on me generously as bread.

I believe that in some way, on that day the air crumbled on me and I saw with an inner eye what cannot be seen, the Eternal, the One in whom we live and move and have our being. I can't prove it, but that and other similar experiences have given me faith and belief that the whole of nature is shot through with a Divine Presence that loves us, holds us, and sustains us in being. We are part of that Divine nature, "partakers of it" to use the biblical phrase (2 Peter 1:4). The written Bible is not the only revelation of God, revelation is all around us. Gerard Manley Hopkins expresses it beautifully in his poem "The Grandeur of God":

The world is charged with the grandeur of God.
It will flame out, like shining from shook foil.

The Esoteric Philosophy considers everything to have an aliveness, an element of consciousness to it, as everything is held in existence by the One Universal Life we call God. There are unseen levels of being, veiled from us most of the time. Maybe in these mystical experiences that so many people have, the veils part for a moment and we touch in on another reality, an experience of unity and oneness that is the true state in which we and everything truly exists.

The Written Word

I believe the Divine Presence is all around and within all creation. God is present before us and within us in an explosion of variety, diversity, beauty and creativity. Concentrating only on the written word as the revelation of God reduces God to what can be fitted in a book – and that attitude has not had a great track record. In the last thousand years, we gave most of our attention to the written biblical revelation, not the bible of nature, and the written word has often been misinterpreted and manipulated for our own self-centred purposes, instead of receiving it with mystery, awe, silence, and surrender – which the natural world demands of us and teaches us. Many have said that a fundamental attitude of awe is the primal religious experience and the beginning of the search for God. Awe is what we often experience in the majesty of nature. I live on the wild and windy West coast of Wales, amidst stunning sunsets, stormy seas and beautiful scenery. Awe is a natural reaction in the face of nature. If there were a religion called "Aweism" we would not waste energy trying to dot every "i" and cross every "t" of doctrine – this religion would be inhabited by people who see that everything in this natural world is amazing, incredible, a miracle of nature, a divine creation. Maybe living as I do on a beautiful peninsula brings that out for me.

Summary

In summary, the Bible is a complex gathering of varied material over a twelve hundred-year time period, written from two to three thousand years ago for a variety of purposes, some of which we might call "spin" these days, composed with a persuasive purpose in mind. It is interpenetrated and influenced by ideas from other faith traditions as well. How the written texts are used often depends on our own level of spiritual development and cultural conditioning. For instance, the treatment of so-called "heretics" or "witches" in the past flagrantly ignored the commandment "Thou shalt not kill." The subjugation of women flies in the face of Genesis 1:27 "God created humankind in his image, in the image of God he created them; male and female he created them." It also does not include any of the many Christian texts that have been rediscovered in recent years, texts that were ruled out in the early days by various influential bishops who shaped the way Christianity was to be formed. Many of these texts are now being re-examined and cast a new light on Christianity altogether. This is the subject of our next two chapters – the "lost Christianities."

Questions for Reflection

1. How do you feel about the statement that the Bible is inerrant?
2. Is the Bible the Word of God, or the word of human beings about God, or both?
3. Are there parts of the Bible with which you feel

uncomfortable or disagree? Which parts? What do you do with that?

4. How have you experienced the Divine Presence in your life? What part has scripture played in that?

Further Study Resources

Armstrong, Karen, 2008. *The Bible: The Biography.* London: Atlantic Books

Spong, John Shelby, 1996. *Liberating the Gospels: Reading the Bible with Jewish Eyes.* San Francisco CA: HarperSanFrancisco

Borg, Marcus, 2003. *The Heart of Christianity: Rediscovering a Life of Faith.* San Francisco CA: HarperSanFrancisco. Chapter Three: "The Bible"

Chapter 2

The Lost Christianities and the Gospel of Thomas

A Tale of Intrigue

Back in the December of 1945, just after the end of the Second World War, some shepherds near Nag Hammadi on the River Nile in Egypt came across a historic find of a large clay jar. On smashing the jar open, they found it was filled with papyri bound in the form of books, called "codices". There are two main versions of the story, but the one told by James M. Robinson is the most entertaining! He conducted interviews over several years with people from the towns and villages around there, and retold the tale spun to him by Muhammad Ali of the al-Summan clan, a resident of al-Qasr. He and his brothers had gone out on their camels, looking for some naturally occurring fertiliser that could be found at the foot of a cliff called Jabal al-Tarif. As they were digging, they came across this large storage jar buried underneath a rock, with its mouth sealed by a lid. Initially they were apprehensive of opening it, as they feared it might contain a *jinn*, or genie, that could cause trouble if released from the jar (as in the story of Aladdin's Lamp!). However, curiosity overcame fear and Muhammad Ali smashed it open with his mattock, and found a collection of what to him were uninteresting old books, more than a dozen old codices bound in golden brown leather.

Thinking they might have some value, Muhammad wrapped the books in his tunic and took them home, to the hamlet of al-Qasr. The books, with loose covers and loose pages, were dumped in the straw, next to the oven. A blood-feud with another family was happening at the time (a fairly common occurrence apparently!) and so Muhammad deposited some of the books with the local Coptic priest, as the police were searching his house almost nightly for weapons. The priest's wife had a brother who went from village to village teaching English and history in the local Coptic Church schools. He came to visit, and, on seeing one of the books, recognised it might be valuable and took it to Cairo. There he showed it to a Coptic physician interested in the Coptic language, who called in the authorities from the Department of Antiquities. They seized the book, giving him a token payment, and the book was deposited in the museum, according to the register, on 4 October 1946.

Meanwhile, thinking the books were worthless, Ali's widowed mother had burned part of those left lying in the straw to help light the oven! Subsequently, by various means, including a certain Bahij 'Ali, the one-eyed outlaw of al-Qasr (you couldn't make it up!), most of the books found their way to Cairo, and eventually into the hands of various dealers in antiquities. After much study and translations by scholars, the texts were slowly returned to Egypt and now are in the Coptic Museum in Cairo.

Out of this tale of discovery and near destruction, what has emerged are thirteen codices on fourth-century papyrus, containing fifty-two texts. There was some repetition, so the number of unique works was forty-five. They had been translated into Coptic from the original Greek and are thought to be the precious texts of an early monastery established by Pachomius – close to the find were the sites of two Pachomian monasteries from the fourth century.

Lost Christianities

These early monasteries were formed from the many men and women that went out into the desert to join St Anthony and the Desert Fathers and Mothers who had spent their lives in contemplation. After a decree by North African Bishop Athanasius in 367 CE that only his list, more or less the canon as we have it now, was to be used, the monks presumably could not bear to destroy their precious, sacred texts, so they hid them as a kind of "time capsule" until the time was right and humanity more receptive to receive them. The Church prides itself on being a single, unbroken line of transmission stretching all the way back to Jesus himself, but scholars now understand that the origins of Christianity were actually marked by considerable diversity and competition, with a variety of early Christian groups who remembered the Jesus event in very different ways. What we now call "orthodoxy" is essentially the viewpoint of the winner, the one that succeeded in crowding all the other parties off the playing field. The contemporary biblical scholar Bart Ehrman has called these unsuccessful competitors *Lost Christianities*, the title of his book, and their voices are now increasingly recognized as holding key pieces of the Jesus story and a more complete understanding of the Jesus teachings themselves. What emerges out of these other texts is a variety of ways of understanding the Jesus event. We are the generation gifted with these texts – but with this goes the responsibility to respond to what they have to say about Christianity. Through these "lost Christianities" we begin to see that Christianity began in pluralism with a whole range of spiritual communities at different levels of awareness and awakening.

Because of the complexities of analysing, translating and interpreting these texts, alongside their controversial nature and the dismissive attitude of many, publication of them took a long time. It wasn't until the early 1970s that English translations became widely available. Several other discoveries have also turned up in the last one hundred and thirty years that also took a long time to be published. In 1896, a codex emerged from Egypt containing the Gospel of Mary, the Acts of Peter, the Secret Book of John and the Wisdom of Jesus Christ. Again, for various reasons, publication of these did not happen until 1955. In 1978 another collection was unearthed in Egypt with several more texts, one of which was the Gospel of Judas, which created a storm when it was published in 2006.

What has become apparent is that the familiar gospels attributed to Matthew, Mark, Luke and John are only a small selection of texts from amongst many differing traditions. (As mentioned earlier, I use the word "attributed" because the traditional authors were only attributed to the gospels about a hundred years after they were written. We don't actually know who wrote them.) Initially, the rediscovered texts were labelled as heresy, a word of Greek derivation that ironically means "choice"! Here are some of the other gospels that have been found.

- The Gospel of Thomas
- The Gospel of Truth
- The Gospel of Philip
- The Gospel of Judas
- The Gospel of Mary (Magdalene)

They have been termed by some the Gnostic Gospels, which is really a misnomer, trying to categorise them into one group. Gnosis simply means "knowledge" or "wisdom". Does gnostic equal non-Christian? No, this idea has been abandoned by most scholars and is seen as an intellectual fiction, an invention to categorise (and thereby demonise by some) texts that challenged the prevailing view of Christianity. It is widely recognised now that there is no such thing as a defined belief of Gnosticism, it was just a convenient catchall invented by those who saw these new texts as an inconvenient truth. They could then lump all of them together to be ignored! However, tables are turning, and it seems to me that the term Gnostic has now morphed into an alternative expression for the perennial wisdom philosophy, which is increasingly being recognised as a viable element within Christianity. Which just goes to show you can't keep a good idea down!

The Gospel of Thomas

The Gospel of Thomas is probably the best known of the texts. It is a collection of one hundred and fourteen sayings attributed to Jesus. There is no narrative story of Jesus' life and death, but it does contain some of the same parables and sayings. It is quintessentially all about how to awaken spiritually and is less concerned with *who* Jesus is than with *how* he calls us to live our lives. When the so-called Gnostic gospels were first discovered the argument made was that they were thought to be written much later and therefore were theologically deficient and contaminated. However, opinions on dating have changed, and more recently scholars have come to believe that the early sayings of the Gospel of Thomas were very early. They may have been copied in the fourth century, but stemmed from much earlier.

One of the experts in this field, Professor April Deconick, has developed the theory of the "rolling Thomas". In her view, the oral sayings of Jesus were gradually collected over a period of time, but much of it comes from 30–50 CE, i.e. much earlier than the canonised gospels, **and even contemporary with the letters of Paul**. Because it is a group of sayings, rather than a narrative story, it is thought to have been added to as time went on, but much of it is probably very early, and reflects the actual words of Jesus more than the canonical gospels. That was a wake-up call for some of us!

Many of the sayings of the Gospel of Thomas are rather cryptic in the sense of making you go beyond analytical reasoning into intuitive mind in order to discern their meaning. They benefit from long reflection to extract the nourishment from them, like a cow chewing the cud. This can lead to enlightenment and a transformation of consciousness. It was a standard way that Jesus taught with parables and cryptic sayings. His oft repeated cry was "Let anyone with ears to hear listen!" As the poet Rainer Maria Rilke implied, the way to wisdom is not by having the right answers, but by asking the right questions.

This style of teaching is a way of perceiving the world that helps us to go beyond the egoic, dualistic mind that thinks in opposites. It takes us from "either-or" thinking to "both-and" thinking. Egoic thinking is at the tribal consciousness level. Many are still stuck in that tribal mentality that says "These are my people, this is my club, this is my country, we are in and you are out." Tribal consciousness is dualistic, it defines borders and barriers to say who is acceptable and who is not. It is basically the root from which all conflicts and wars come from. It is, to quote the American Franciscan priest Fr Richard Rohr, "stinkin' thinkin'"! The sayings of the Gospel of Thomas try to help us to transcend that. They are intended to circumvent that busy, calculating-and-planning egoic brain that dominates personality thinking and drop us straight into the higher mind at soul level, the centre of our being, where it becomes possible to weigh the deeper questions of meaning and purpose. In a way, they hold a mirror to our own lives and invite us to look deeper within. Jesus was essentially teaching us to change the way we think.

Here is a small sample of the sayings, with my own understanding of their meaning, gleaned from various sources. Translations are from the version by Stephen Patterson and Marvin Meyer, freely available on the internet.

Saying One

1. These are the secret sayings that the living Jesus spoke and Didymos Judas Thomas recorded. And he said, "Whoever discovers the interpretation of these sayings will not taste death."

Didymos Judas Thomas. There is a strange thing here. Didymos is the Greek for twin. In Aramaic, the language Jesus spoke, Thomas also means twin, so there is a double twin statement at the beginning, "Twin Judas twin!" What was being implied here? In some circles, particularly Syriac Christianity, Judas is thought to possibly be the twin brother of Jesus, or maybe one of a pair of twins in Jesus' family. In the disciple's group, maybe this Judas was just called by his nickname "Twin" which is "Thomas" in Aramaic, to distinguish him from the other Judas (Iscariot). The Gospel of Mark lists James and Judas as Jesus' brothers. Maybe this Judas was the one called "doubting Twin" after the resurrection appearances.

Or, alternatively, could "twinness" be a symbol for something? Are we to "twin" with Jesus and become one with him? Is there a joining, a merging to happen on the path of transformation? It's all hinting at the purpose of the gospel – to get us to think and move on, to awaken to a different view. Maybe it's about twinning with the inner Christ, the divine within, being joined up internally. It certainly seems to be a theme running through the Gospel of Thomas. It can, of course, contain both meanings.

Secret sayings. Nowadays secret means something held back or not shared, but not in first-century Aramaic. It is the same word as in "pray in secret to your heavenly Father" in Matthew chapter 6, i.e. in an inner place. Its root meaning is inner or hidden. Things can be hidden in plain sight if our attention is in the wrong place. We need a certain state of consciousness to see and hear it (Jesus: "Let anyone with ears to hear listen!").

Whoever discovers the interpretation of these sayings will not taste death. Discovering is about recognition. There is a distinction between seeing something and recognising it. Recognition is allowing something to enter into one's being, it is waking up to something new. "Will not taste death" is to be freed from the bitter taste of death. As someone said, "If death of the body happens before death of the ego, God help you!" If you know you are ultimately one with everything in a timeless existence, death has no hold, no fear, as there is no death, just continuity of existence in another realm. Discover that interpretation of reality and you will not taste death. As I have sometimes said, "I have no fear of death, it's just that I'm not too keen on the process of dying." When we realise and absorb that death is a transition stage rather than an end, we shall not taste death.

Saying Two

2. *Jesus said, "Those who seek should not stop seeking until they find. When they find, they will be disturbed. When they are disturbed, they will marvel, and will reign over all."*

This is to do with paradigms, the lenses through which we view the world. *Paradigm malaise* is when a prevailing worldview becomes stressed and strained, because certain things don't fit it any more. Paradigm malaise begins unconsciously, then all of a sudden a crisis appears, and paradigm breakdown happens. This causes confusion and disturbance. Then a new way of seeing gradually emerges in our consciousness until a transformation happens. Our confusion gives way to the new paradigm, and wonder ensues, we enter into a wider space where we marvel at the new realisation. We can be initially misunderstood and even ostracised or penalised for seeing things differently – or, in the case of Jesus, crucified.

Paradigm malaise is happening big-time in the world today. Existing institutions are straining and cracking apart. The Covid-19 pandemic, happening as I write, means that societal norms which have worked for years are crumbling. New ways forward have to be found. Some people do not like or dare not risk giving up their old worldview to find the new one and they become more and more crystallised and defensive of the old way. We can tie ourselves up with our ideas and attitudes and theologies so that we cannot move with the flow of divine beingness, we cannot adapt to change. As the saying goes, "Most people would prefer to be transformed without having to change."

Sadly, much Church theology has become stuck in the defensive mode, rather than looking for expansive ways forward. As I keep saying, the wisdom philosophy provides a framework that I believe helps us to move on into a better future, if we can realise that we are all on the path of spiritual development at different stages. Much of the suffering we undergo is a call for us to awaken, to open our eyes to a different paradigm and move on as a human race into a more compassionate world, the ideal of which was called "the kingdom of God" by Jesus.

Those who seek should not stop seeking until they find. This has a similar sense to the saying of Jesus in the New Testament "Ask, and it will be given you; search, and you will find; knock, and the door will be opened for you" (Matthew 7:7). Opening the door is stepping out into that place of wonder and marvel, a new understanding. What is emphasized is the need for perseverance – keep on ruminating on it all until the mists clear and a new horizon comes into view. Saying 92 has a similar sense: "Seek and you will find. In the past, however, I did not tell you the things about which you asked me then. Now I am willing to tell them, but you are not seeking them."

As I said, I am writing this in the middle of the Covid-19 pandemic. What is noticeable at present is that new ideas are bubbling up all around the world, as if the blinkers have been taken off and many are looking for a new start. It is a time of change and opportunities for transformation. As we realise the old ways are no longer working, no longer serving the purpose they were meant to serve, so radical ideas spring forth from the imaginal, intuitive level of the soul. New ways forward for societies. New paradigms in science, new economics and politics. Albert Einstein's quotation, though maybe overused, is very relevant for these times, "We can't solve problems by using the same kind of thinking we used when we created them." We have to move up a level, or to use St Paul's words, "Be transformed by the renewing of your minds" (Romans 12:2).

They will marvel, and will reign over all. What power is released in marvelling? If we lose our sense of separate self, and gain the sense of solidarity in that we human beings are all in this together, we gain the power of freedom, we are no longer held back by the way in which we used to see the world. We are set free! "Then Jesus said to the Jews who had believed in him, 'If you continue in my word, you are truly my disciples; and you will know the truth, and the truth will make you free'" (John 8:31–32).

In the famous Hindu text the Bhagavad Gita, one interpretation is that Arjuna, the charioteer, is the Soul, the five horses are the senses. The charioteer should be in charge, not the senses. The whole of the Gospel of Thomas is about moving the centre of consciousness from the ego-desire-self (the horses), to the true self (the charioteer). Then we are set free! The Sufi poet Rumi said, "Sell your cleverness and buy bewilderment." Being bewildered allows one to take on board new ways of seeing and expand into greater awareness. It is the beginnings of a paradigm shift, and an evolution in consciousness, a new awakening.

Saying Three

3. *Jesus said, "If your leaders say to you, 'Look, the (Father's) kingdom is in the sky,' then the birds of the sky will precede you. If they say to you, 'It is in the sea,' then the fish will precede you. Rather, the kingdom is within you and it is outside you. When you know yourselves, then you will be known, and you will understand that you are children of the living Father. But if you do not know yourselves, then you live in poverty, and you are the poverty."*

29

The first part of this could be a rephrase by Jesus of Deuteronomy 30:11–14:

Now what I am commanding you today is not too difficult for you or beyond your reach. It is not up in heaven, so that you have to ask, "Who will ascend into heaven to get it and proclaim it to us so we may obey it?" Nor is it beyond the sea, so that you have to ask, "Who will cross the sea to get it and proclaim it to us so we may obey it?" No, the word is very near you; it is in your mouth and in your heart so you may obey it. (Deuteronomy 30:11–14)

One of the biggest hurdles to overcome in the "popular" view of Christianity is that heaven is a place up above where God lives, which seems very unreal in modern times. The Gospel of Thomas emphasises that Divine Presence is both within and all around, not distant and up there. Jesus makes that quite clear in Luke 17:21 when he said the kingdom of God is both within and around us – the word used has both meanings. In a way, this is talking about the direction of our attention. In an immature spiritual state, the attention is always directed outwards to distract oneself from facing the difficulties of the inner self – we are diverted from finding the place of the Divine dwelling within and from facing our own shadow. This has to be taken in hand before the journey really begins. We have to move within and find the inner experience, know the inner self, face the inner shadow. This is the inner, contemplative path. Following this means our actions and all our "doing" can stem from our "being" in Divine Presence. It is following Jesus's teaching to "love your neighbour *as yourself*." This is why being at ease with quiet, silence and solitude and developing a meditative practice is so important for the spiritual journey.

Contemplative prayer or meditation is a vital part in developing this internal awareness. It is part of the Christian heritage and has been practised by monks and nuns down through the years. As Jesus said, "Whenever you pray, go into your room and shut the door and pray to your Father who is in secret; and your Father who sees in secret will reward you" (Matthew 6:6). In this passage, secret has the meaning of hidden. The Divine is hidden within the inner room, and we have to seek. It was the instruction to the hermit monks in the desert: "Sit in your cell and it will teach you everything." It is about developing the capacity to live in our own skin with self-acceptance. This means facing our darker sides, understanding ourselves with all our imperfections. If we cannot accept who we are, it is a huge stumbling block that will trip us up continually. We need self-acceptance and understanding in order to move forward. To know your true self is to know you have a divine essence, that you are held in being, at one with the One Beingness that holds everything. The true self is not just a cleaned up version of our usual neurotic self, it is Self at a higher level, with more compassion, wisdom, intuition, and love. As Socrates is quoted as saying, "To know thyself is the beginning of wisdom."

* * *

So Divine reality, or the kingdom, is inside and all around. In fact, modern physics tells us that the inside and the outside are all one energetic continuum. Our essence of energy extends way out beyond our bodies, it is all around. The "beyond" is all interconnected with what is here in the eternal Oneness of Creation. Every moment is full of divine reality. There is only one universe and it is like a Mobius strip, the inside and outside are one. It is an illusion that the inside and outside are separate.

I used to teach science, and sometimes got whole classes making Mobius strips, mainly because I was fascinated by it myself. You take a strip of paper, which obviously has two surfaces and two edges. Then you twist it once, and join the ends. It looks like it still has two surfaces and two edges, but if you follow a surface or an edge around, you soon realise that, despite what you think you can see with your eyes, it has only one edge and one surface. The inside is the outside, they are one. Slightly baffling, but demonstrably true!

The Mobius Strip

Saying Four

4. Jesus said, "The person old in days won't hesitate to ask a little child seven days old about the place of life, and that person will live. For many of the first will be last, and will become a single one."

The person old in days. Those of great age were considered to be of greater wisdom as well, people to be listened to, respected as an elder with life experience.

A little child seven days old. What does it evoke? A new-born baby – helpless, vulnerable, innocent and dependent. There is no sense of being an individual in a new-born, they are still one with their mother, their source. Why seven days old? In Hebrew numerology, seven indicated perfection and wholeness (see Chapter 6). In Judaism, on the eighth day, the child was taken in to the temple and circumcised. How do we ask an infant about life? Who is the infant? Is it our own inner child, our original innocence, our naked soul? So here it is saying that if we have wisdom, we will seek illumination from our Soul, the treasure in the field and the pearl of greatest price in another parable.

For many of the first will be last, and will become a single one. When are the first and the last right next to each other? In a whole circle, there is no first or last, it is all one, united.

This saying is about awakening to the oneness of All, attaining unitive consciousness. We are there in it as infants and before birth. There is no sense of being an individual in a new-born. There is a symbiosis between mother and infant – they are one. A new-born has no sense of "self". As we grow, we separate out, become dual in our awareness. The ego, necessary for our development, soon begins to form and operate and we fall into the illusion of separateness and duality. We fall "asleep". The journey is back to the state of wakefulness, non-dual awareness, rediscovering that which has always been within us. The first and last are the same when a circle is formed, creating wholeness.

The same sense is conveyed in the words of Jesus in Mark's gospel:

> *He sat down, called the twelve, and said to them, "Whoever wants to be first must be last of all and servant of all." Then he took a little child and put it among them; and taking it in his arms, he said to them, "Whoever welcomes one such child in my name welcomes me, and whoever welcomes me welcomes not me but the one who sent me." Mark 9:35–37*

I could continue, but we begin to get the idea of this form of teaching. It makes us ask questions and to think deeply and work things out for ourselves. This was not popular with the increasing authority of the bishops in the Church, and it was little wonder that Athanasius did not include it in his declared authoritative list in 367 CE. They couldn't have people thinking for themselves, they had to do what they were told! That was what the Roman Empire needed – obedient citizens. However, thinking for oneself was exactly the radical and challenging nature of Jesus' teaching, which was why the authorities then wanted to do away with him. If any single text from the Nag Hammadi discoveries should be included in the Bible, it should be the Gospel of Thomas.

Transformation Not Transaction

Essentially, the Gospel of Thomas, much of which recalls the original words of Jesus, teaches a path of transformation, not transaction. Jesus teaches a way of rising above the lower, self-centred nature which operates out of the personality's desires and wants. He seeks to reorient us in a higher Self, which operates from a place of non-judgementalism, understanding and compassion, teaching us how to love our neighbour and ourselves. He did not tell us that his death was in order to pay off the debt to a judgemental Father God. That was the transactional direction the early Church took after 325 CE as it grew in power and control and affiliation with the Roman Empire, seeking to provide a means for the Empire to unite its diverse populace. The deal offered to the populace was "Believe in Jesus and enter into the transaction of his sacrifice in this life and you will get to heaven – you are saved!" The main emphasis of Jesus was sidelined, because his teaching was to think for ourselves, to change and transform our inner nature and operate from the authority of our Highest Self, our Soul, not beholden to any earthly authority. "Render unto Caesar the things that are Caesar's; and unto God the things that are God's" (Matthew 22:21 RV). That was not acceptable to the Roman Church, beholden as they were to the Roman authorities. Such radicalism, teaching people to think for themselves, was not conducive to maintaining order in the populace of the Empire.

Hal Taussig, a professor of biblical literature and early Christianity, places the Gospel of Thomas at the beginning of his *A New New Testament* as reading it enables us to see how many of these sayings were woven into the stories of the narrative gospels of Mark, Matthew and Luke – many, but by no means all, as some demand considerable thought and presumably could not be fitted into the narrative, even if the authors of the gospels knew of them at all. Reading Thomas requires some insight into many of the key words and phrases, and here is my own understanding of some of them, which may be helpful if you choose to delve into Thomas:

- **Cosmos:** this Greek word is used in the Coptic text, and is taken to mean the human world in which we live, often in a negative way.
- **Clothes:** the outer appearance, or the realm of human activity.
- **Dead, asleep, drunk:** those who are not spiritually awakened.
- **Infant:** may represent the soul, a state of innocence and wholeness.
- **Naked:** casting off the clothes, the outer appearance, revealing the true Self/Soul.
- **Oneness, United:** the state of being unified with the soul, awake, at one, non-dual consciousness. Twoness is being in duality, divided, self-centred, egoic.
- **Secret:** hidden, something in the inner place, e.g., Matthew 6 "pray in secret to your heavenly Father."
- **Seven:** representing wholeness, completeness, perfection.
- **Sleep:** the state of inner spiritual blindness.
- **To stand to one's feet:** maturity, alert and awake, not drunk or asleep – to reorient one's conscious awareness – metanoia (repentance).

Summary

The Gospel of Thomas presents us with some of the earliest recorded sayings of Jesus, many of which are not recorded in the four traditional gospels. As such it is of vital importance for Christians in following the teachings of Jesus. Unfortunately,

Church authorities have not yet allowed it to be used within services of worship, so it is little known amongst those who simply get their teaching by attending church services. Its emphasis is to think for ourselves and to work out the meaning of the texts as they apply to our lives, much in the same way as Jesus told his parables. In this it is a timeless presentation of wisdom teaching, helping us to own our inner shadow selves and progress along the path of transformation, as taught by Jesus and presented in the Perennial Wisdom teachings.

Questions for Reflection

1. What is stopping the Church from incorporating some of the new scriptural discoveries?
2. Transformation or transaction? Which do you see as the teaching of Jesus?
3. Why are so many of Jesus' teachings in parables and pithy statements?
4. In what ways does the discovery of the Gospel of Thomas add to your understanding of Jesus' teaching?

Further Study Resources

Baumann, Lynn C., Baumann Ward J., Bourgeault, Cynthia, 2008. *The Luminous Gospels: Thomas, Mary Magdalene and Philip.* Texas: Praxis Publishing

Ehrman, Bart D., 2003. *Lost Christianities: The Battles for Scripture and the Faith We Never Knew.* New York: Oxford University Press

Meyer, Marvin (ed.), 2007. *The Nag Hammadi Scriptures: The International Edition.* New York: HarperCollins

Pagels, Elaine, 2004. *Beyond Belief: The Secret Gospel of Thomas.* London: Pan MacMillan

Chapter Three

The Lost Christianities and Mary Magdalene

Many of the recently discovered texts are only partial, with pages or sections missing, due to wear and tear and various insects' appetites! But some are very significantly whole and cast new light on the established New Testament texts. Professor Hal Taussig, as mentioned in the previous chapter, has created *A New New Testament: A Bible for the Twenty-first Century Combining Traditional and Newly Discovered Texts,* in which he has added ten new books from the early Christ movements. It has been produced in collaboration with a host of biblical scholars and historians. Alongside the existing traditional literature, these new writings, he says, "sparkle with fresh comparisons and contrasts". In addition to the twenty-six canonical books of the New Testament, his version includes:

- The Prayer of Thanksgiving – placed right at the beginning
- The Gospel of Thomas – placed before the other gospels
- The Odes of Solomon – divided into three sections throughout
- The Thunder: Perfect Mind – an unusual text with the overall message *I am everything*
- The Gospel of Mary – placed after John's gospel
- The Gospel of Truth
- The Prayer of the Apostle Paul
- The Acts of Paul and Thecla
- The Letter of Peter to Philip
- The Secret Revelation of John

In the preface, Taussig says:

The New New Testament opens the door to reciting the Sermon on the Mount alongside the Gospel of Mary, in which Mary Magdalene courageously comforts all the disciples and teaches them things Jesus had taught only her. In addition to the traditional Revelation to John, it offers a very different Secret Revelation of John in which Christ also rescues the world from a vicious empire, not by end-of-the-world battles and curses that set the earth on fire, but by straightforward teaching about God's light and compassion.... It is not time to throw out the traditional New Testament, or to excise those parts that offend. Rather, the moment has arrived to add to it and rebind it.

Mary Magdalene

History has always been written by the winners and, as most of those have been male, it has been "his-story" rather than "her-story". One particular person who has suffered from that truth is Mary Magdalene, whose prominent place amongst the apostles gradually was written out until she was finally demonised as a prostitute, due to Pope Gregory I in 591 CE. He merged Mary Magdalene with Mary of Bethany and also the unnamed "sinful woman" who anoints Jesus' feet in Luke 7. Whilst Mary Magdalene and Mary of Bethany may indeed be the same person, the inclusion of the "sinful woman" resulted in a widespread but inaccurate belief that she was a repentant prostitute or promiscuous woman. This wasn't rebutted until 1969, over one thousand years later, by Pope Paul VI. Hence, in popular culture and musicals such as *Jesus Christ Superstar* she is still seen as a repentant prostitute, with no justification in scripture. The lost Christianities give us a startling new picture and show us something of the place of Mary Magdalene amongst the apostles, and it is very different from the "repentant prostitute" version that the Church supported for centuries.

The Gospel of Mary Magdalene indicates that Mary was the person close to Jesus who really understood his message, more so than the other apostles. Church historians place it between 80 and 180 CE, some believing it is contemporary with the Gospel of Luke. Mary was, in effect, the "Apostle to the Apostles" (a title given to her recently by the Roman Catholic Church, because she was the one who brought the message of the empty tomb to the apostles). From the Gospel of Mary we see that she was also the one to whom Jesus gave the inner meanings of his teaching. It is sadly only a partial gospel, as much of it has been lost, eaten and disintegrated over the years. Even so, we read:

> Peter turned to her and said, "Sister we know that the Savior greatly loved you above all women, so tell us what you remember of his words that we ourselves do not know or perhaps have never heard." Mary replied: "I will tell you, then, as much as I know of what may be hidden or unknown to you." (Baumann 2008 p. 67)

She goes on to begin to describe a vision of the Lord that she had, but then, sadly, several pages are missing. It picks up again at the end of Mary's discourse and then she lapses into silence. At that point, Andrew expresses his worries about the strangeness of the teaching and Peter then criticises Mary and puts her down, saying,

> Would the Savior speak these things to a woman in private without openly sharing them so that we too might hear? Should we listen to her at all, and did he choose her over us because she is more worthy than we are? (Baumann 2008 p. 69)

Mary then weeps and defends herself and Levi (aka Matthew) speaks up for her, saying,

> You have always been quick to anger, Peter, and now you are questioning her in exactly the same manner, treating this woman as if she were an enemy. If the Savior considered her worthy, who are

you to reject her? He knew her completely and loved her faithfully.
We should be ashamed of ourselves! (Baumann 2008 p. 69)

So here we see a gospel in which Mary Magdalene is clearly seen by the other apostles as the one who really got it, and was respected by some of them for that. However, we also see the beginnings of the downplaying of her part and the rivalry from Peter, who felt usurped in his place as a leader of the apostles. This was the beginning of the marginalisation of her place in the other gospels.

Mary the True Disciple

There are many hints in other texts that Mary was the one who truly understood the message of Jesus. In the Dialogue of the Saviour, she is characterised as "a woman who understood everything." In the Pistis Sophia, thought to be a third-century text, Jesus says to Mary,

Blessed Mary, you whom I shall complete with all the mysteries on high, speak openly, for you are one whose heart is set on heaven's kingdom more than all your brothers. (Meyer 2004, p. 66)

Mary, you are more blessed than all the women on earth, because you will be the fullness of fullnesses and the completion of completions. (Meyer, 2004 p. 67)

We also see again Peter's antagonism towards Mary:

My master, we cannot endure this woman who gets in our way and does not let any of us speak, though she talks all the time. (Meyer, 2004 p. 68)

This vehemence towards Mary by Peter is also shown at the end of the Gospel of Thomas, where the last saying is a puzzling one as Jesus appears to deny the value of femaleness:

> *Simon Peter said to them, "Mary should leave us, for females are not worthy of life." Jesus said, "Look, I shall make her male, so that she too may become a living spirit resembling you males. For every female who makes herself male will enter heaven's kingdom."* (Meyer, 2004 p. 35)

On the face of it, that is a shocker from Jesus! But Professor Marvin Meyer, the translator, explains:

> *Commonly, in antiquity, the female is made to symbolize what is earthly and perishable and the male what is heavenly and imperishable. If that is also the case here, then the transformation of the female into the male impacts all people, women and men, who seek to leave what is perishable and attain what is imperishable. Then what is true for Mary becoming male is true for all people, whatever their gender, who participate in femaleness. The world of perishability is overcome, the dying cosmos of the mother goddess is transcended, and she – and all human beings who are physical and earthly – can be transformed to the spiritual and heavenly. (Meyer, 2004 p. 25)*

This is a version of the perennial wisdom teachings, where the Christ is the mediating Love principle between the masculine aspect of Divine Will and feminine aspect of the Divine Creative Intelligence. All that has been emanated into existence is eventually brought back into the One Source, and male and female become one. It is the movement spoken of by Paul, "For this perishable body must put on imperishability, and this mortal body must put on immortality" (1 Corinthians 15:53).

Jesus' Companion?

The Gospel of Philip, contains these two startling texts:

Three women always walked with the Master: Mary his mother, his sister, and Mary Magdalene who is called his companion. For "Mary" is the name of his sister, his mother, and his companion. (Meyer 2004 p. 44)

The companion of the Anointed One was Miriam of Magdala, for the Master appeared to love her more than the other students, and many times would kiss her on her [mouth]. The other disciples said to him, "Why do you love her more than all of us?" (Meyer 2004 p. 49)

The use of the word *companion* could mean just as his spiritual companion, the one who understood him. The word that has been rendered as "mouth" is in square brackets, meaning that it was missing; there was a hole in the papyrus. Presumably it could also have said cheek, head or hands, but translators seem to prefer mouth from the context. The implication is really that she was not just his spiritual companion, but his sexual companion.

Whether we believe that or not, it does raise some serious questions. Are we allowed to think that Jesus might have been married? It would have been normal for a Jewish man of his age. Does he have to have been celibate? How did that notion arise? Did he have children? These tantalising questions have been the fodder of much sensationalism and several novels, but there is ultimately no way of knowing, unless further texts come to light and are proven to be authentic. What these many rediscovered texts do show us is that the growing Church, dominated by male figures, progressively challenged and sidelined female involvement until we reached the situation where Jesus was a celibate male, which became the model for Roman Catholic priests, despite it being fairly obvious in the letters of Paul and in the Acts of the Apostles that several women were leaders in the very early church.

The recent discoveries of these new texts challenge male

patriarchy and the view that spiritual authority lies in "maleness". This is a misunderstanding of the teachings of antiquity, the perennial wisdom teachings, in which the ultimate Divine Source is both male and female, the male aspect being the Will-to-Be, the driving energy of life, and the female aspect is the Will-to-Create, the energy to bring form into manifestation. These two aspects, in relationship with each other, give birth to the Will-to-Love, the consciousness pervading the universe and bringing self-awareness – and so we get a Divine Trinity of energies emanating from the One Source. A Trinity of Divine Will, Divine Love, and Divine Creative Intelligence. This is a deep teaching which is expanded in many texts that stem in their inspiration from the subtle realms. The Christian Holy Trinity is but one expression of the underlying truth, as is the trinity of Shiva, Vishnu and Brahma in Hinduism, the Three Bodies of Buddhahood in Buddhism, and the Three Pure Ones in Taoism. (More on the Perennial Wisdom teachings in a later book in this Wisdom series.)

What Happened to Mary Magdalene?

In the West, the main story is that she travelled to France in a boat with Mary, mother of Jesus, Lazarus and others (in some versions she is pregnant with the child of Jesus) and lived out a hermit life in a cave for 30 years before dying at the Chapel of Saint-Maximin, about 75 miles northeast of Marseille, in the Southeast of France. In the Eastern Orthodox traditions, Mary is believed to have left Jerusalem with Mary, mother of Jesus, and travelled to Ephesus, in modern-day Turkey where she eventually died. Neither of them have much substantiation, so we really do not know.

However, I recently came across a publication by Jehanne de Quillan entitled *The Gospel of the Beloved Companion: The Complete Gospel of Mary Magdalene* which puts forward the idea that the author of the fourth gospel was not John but Mary Magdalene who was the "beloved disciple" mentioned numerous times in the gospel. This is based on a text that is said to have been handed down for generations amongst families in the Languedoc area of France, reputedly brought from Alexandria in the middle part of the first century and translated from Greek into Occitan in the twelfth century. The actual document has not been released to the examination of scholars, as those who have guarded it for centuries do not permit its scrutiny. The book presents what purports to be the original gospel of John before it was redacted and amended by later hands, plus the full Gospel of Mary, including all the missing sections from the existing text. It is a fascinating read, giving a slightly different slant to the fourth gospel, which incorporates some of the sayings in the Gospel of Thomas. The missing sections from the Gospel of Mary give us a mystical teaching about the tree of life which the soul has to ascend in a series of initiations. There is no proof at all of its authenticity and provenance, but it certainly gives much food for thought!

In Conclusion

Imagine for a moment – what would Christianity be like if Mary Magdalene had been seen as the rightful leader of the church, the one who was to take it forward after the death of Jesus? How would it have developed if Peter had taken a back seat and allowed Mary to head up the Jerusalem Church? Would it have survived and flourished? Would the teaching have been different? Realistically, at the time, it was probably impossible, given that Judaism was thoroughly patriarchal in its leadership, as was the cruel and dominating Roman Empire. However, we now have the insight and awareness to see that God is neither male nor female, but contains both aspects. If only the Church could recognise that more in its liturgy and doctrine! The Holy Spirit could become the female creative aspect and the Christ the loving consciousness created throughout the universe. Now, in this time of rising gender equality and the ebbing of patriarchy, the teachings within Christianity that were given to Mary Magdalene to continue with can come out into the open. Those teachings are contained within the Perennial Wisdom and are about human spiritual transformation via a series of gradual step-changes in consciousness.

Questions for Reflection

1. How does it impact on your spirituality to think that Mary Magdalene was the disciple who understood the message of Jesus, and possibly his companion spiritually, if not sexually?
2. What difficulties do you find with the patriarchal nature of Christianity?
3. Does it make any difference to your faith if Jesus was not celibate?
4. How can the feminine be integrated into modern Church life and belief?

Further Study Resources

Bourgeault, Cynthia, 2010. *The Meaning of Mary Magdalene: Discovering the Woman at the Heart of Christianity.* Boston MA: Shambhala Publications

De Quillan, Jehanne, 2011. *The Gospel of the Beloved Companion: The Complete Gospel of Mary Magdalene.* North Charleston CA: Create Space

Lester, Meera, 2006. *The Everything Mary Magdalene Book: the life and legacy of Jesus' most misunderstood disciple.* Avon MA: Adams Media

Meyer, Marvin, 2004. *The Gospels of Mary: The Secret Tradition of Mary Magdalene the Companion of Jesus.* New York: HarperCollins

Taussig, Hal (ed.), 2015. *A New New Testament: A Bible for the 21st Century.* New York: Houghton Mifflin Harcourt Publishing Co

Websites

https://departments.kings.edu/womens_history/marymagda.html This
gives a good overview of the Mary Magdalene controversies
with many links to other sites and books

Chapter Four

The Hard Problem of Interpretation

Should we interpret the Bible literally, i.e. believing in the literal meaning of every word, phrase and sentence as stated on the page? Many Christians do exactly that, which often gives Christianity a bad name because of their intransigence, especially over issues such as Creation and the Virgin Birth. Here are some biblical problems with that way of looking at it.

On the day when the LORD gave the Amorites over to the Israelites, Joshua spoke to the LORD; and he said in the sight of Israel, "Sun, stand still at Gibeon, and Moon, in the valley of Aijalon." And the sun stood still, and the moon stopped, until the nation took vengeance on their enemies. Is this not written in the Book of Jashar? The sun stopped in mid-heaven, and did not hurry to set for about a whole day. (Joshua 10:12–13)

If the sun stood still, i.e. if the earth stopped spinning, tectonic plates would collide and a cataclysm would be released via violent weather, earthquakes, volcanoes, tsunamis, etc. The resultant cloud cover would mean worldwide crop failure and freezing temperatures. Humanity and much other life would probably be wiped out. It would also defy the laws of physics. It is just not possible.

If your right eye causes you to sin, tear it out and throw it away; it is better for you to lose one of your members than for your whole body to be thrown into hell. And if your right hand causes you to sin, cut it off and throw it away; it is better for you to lose one of your members than for your whole body to go into hell. (Matthew 5:29–30)

There would be a lot of one-eyed, one-handed Christians if that were taken literally! Why do we not take that literally? The very next verse in Matthew is about divorce and adultery, which has been taken literally, causing great upset and trauma to many. What judgement do we use to decide which verses to interpret literally? The verse below is certainly not one to hold to.

No one whose testicles are crushed or whose penis is cut off shall be admitted to the assembly of the LORD. (Deuteronomy 23:1)

Try policing that one in Church! In their culture, for some reason they did not want eunuchs in the temple. Today, enforcement of that "law" would be totally unthinkable. So what decides whether we take a text literally or not?

The Problem

These three quotations above illustrate different problems. The first flies in the face of science, the second is that it is not good common sense to maim oneself, and the third is well, a cultural problem, say no more! We cannot say the Bible is literally true if we then ignore much of it because to follow the literal instructions would be foolhardy, ridiculous or cruel. There has to be interpretation by recognising the time, context and culture in which it was written, and an understanding of the problems of translation. Historian Karen Armstrong, in her book *The Bible: The Bibliography* (p. 3), notes that an exclusively literal interpretation of the Bible is a recent development.

Until the nineteenth century, very few people imagined that the first chapter of Genesis was a factual account of the origins of life. For centuries, Jews and Christians relished highly allegorical and inventive exegesis, insisting that a wholly literal reading of the Bible was neither possible nor desirable.

The process of interpretation is inevitably affected by a combination of the writer's own personality and the thought-world of the times in which they live. Some biblical stories challenge that thought-world. For example, Job lived in a world which held that God always rewards the just and punishes the unjust, but his own experience showed him that bad things can happen to good people. As the children's rhyme goes, "The rain it raineth on the just, and also on the unjust fella. But mostly on the just because the unjust stole the just's umbrella!"

A Different Culture

Other stories simply agree with the thought-world of the time: for example, the Israelites believed Yahweh was the God of their tribe alone, and therefore it was alright for their God to order the genocide of the other tribes in the promised land of Canaan. It was seen as God's command to kill them all.

> But as for the towns of these peoples that the LORD your God is giving you as an inheritance, you must not let anything that breathes remain alive. You shall annihilate them—the Hittites and the Amorites, the Canaanites and the Perizzites, the Hivites and the Jebusites—just as the LORD your God has commanded. (Deuteronomy 20:16–17)

The Book of Joshua relates how he went ahead in his murderous spree for years, annihilating any opposition. There were other behaviours, accepted then, yet rejected now. In those times, polygamy was not seen as a problem: to have lots of wives was seen as a sign of wealth and of God's blessing. Slavery was accepted as the norm, influencing culture right up to the nineteenth century. The Hebrew Scriptures also contain many instructions to do with dietary regulations, which were necessary in a hot climate before refrigerators were invented, but do not apply in other areas of the world, or in your own kitchen fridge.

Once we accept the view that much of the Bible is a product of the worldview of its time, we have to find another way of finding what values and ideas are authentic. What values do we want to live by in the twenty-first century? In a number of places in the Hebrew Scriptures, the writers indicate that the moral law is "written on our hearts". We have an inner potential to discern what is life-affirming and what is life-denying, and what the basic values are from which we derive our sense of what is good and what is bad. However, we also have a huge capacity to get locked into ideas we feel we "ought" to hold, because, for example, they are our tradition, or everyone we know apparently holds them, or the penalty for not holding them is ostracisation. The path of inner transformation involves recognising our attachments to those old thought-forms and loosening them so that we are free to use our inner organ of spiritual discernment.

Losing Literalism

The literal way of looking at scripture, seeing it all as God-inspired and therefore literally true, has become a barrier to many Christians who find it hard to escape that way of thinking. It has a harder form and a softer form. The harder form of biblical literalism is the insistence that everything the Bible says is the absolute will of God, and that if it said something happened, then that thing really happened. The earth and everything in it really was made in six days. Moses really did part the Red Sea. The sun really did stand still for Joshua. We may have picked up that understanding as children, but for most of us, those arguments simply stopped being persuasive at some stage. Many of us will have a softer form of literalism, seeing some things as actual events and some as mythical stories, and some as interpretations relevant to the culture and context they were written in, which we would understand differently now. The harder form sees the Bible as a divine product, dictated by God and therefore infallible and inerrant. The softer form of literalism says that the biblical writers were guided by the Holy Spirit and therefore there are no serious mistakes in it.

In terms of authority, the harder form would say that evolutionary theory is wrong because it conflicts with the biblical version of creation. The softer form would accept the Creation stories as myth but containing truths, but would consider the New Testament miracles to have taken place much as described. I admit that this was my own view at the beginning of my Christian journey.

The more developed way of looking at the Bible is to consider the various methods of interpretation. The Bible is a product of early ancient communities, and tells us not what God thinks and says, but what those early ancient communities thought about God. It tells us their stories about God, what they thought God was like, and what they thought they had to do to please God. As such, it is a valuable resource for us to understand how humanity's relationship to what it has perceived as the Divine Source has changed over millennia.

Early Apostolic Church Fathers (100–451 CE) recognized that Scripture had four layers of interpretation. The first layer was the literal meaning. The second was allegorical, looking for symbolic meanings in the text. The third they called tropical/moral, looking for broader moral lessons, and the fourth was anagogical, the mystical, metaphorical sense. Often numbers were used symbolically to indicate certain truths, and we shall look at some instances of that later in Chapter 6. The literal level was only ever seen as a surface layer, not to be concentrated on. The deeper transformational meanings came at deeper levels.

In terms of interpreting these writings today, we are now in a position to take a historical-metaphorical approach. Historically, we can ask the question "What did these texts mean in their ancient context and how does that apply today?" This helps us to see their relevance and also their shortcomings. Metaphorically, we can ask "Is there a more-than literal, more-than factual meaning to these stories? Can we find meaning that goes beyond and deeper than any literal interpretation?" The way we treat the parables of Jesus can be extended to reading the rest of the Bible. We know the parables of Jesus are not literally true, they are stories to illustrate a point. We also know there are valuable truths within them. The parables are stories about things that never were, but always are.

Extend that line of thinking to the rest of the Bible – does it matter that some of the stories told about characters in the Bible did not actually happen? It is the meaning of the stories that is important, not whether they literally happened. Some did, some didn't – does it really matter? Does Noah have to be real? Did Moses really part the Red Sea? Did the walls of Jericho really fall down? Did Jonah really survive three days inside a large fish? Reading the Bible with a historical-metaphorical framework is to recognise that it is full of parable-like, truth-filled stories that are told because they are full of meaning for those who wrote them and hopefully for us as well. Whether they all happened exactly like that or not does not really matter. As the Native American elder said before speaking his traditional stories, "Now I don't know whether it happened this way, but I know it's true." The rubber hits the road when we start asking that about the miracles (or signs) of Jesus. Could he have had the ability to walk on water, to heal, to indicate exactly where a huge catch of fish could be found – or are these stories trying to convey something deeper and symbolic about the nature of Jesus?

We probably all swing between these different ways of interpreting scripture. I see the Bible very much as showing us a gradual growth in the people's understanding of what God is really like, especially in the stories in the Hebrew Scriptures. They were written in a context and culture very different from ours, and we can't really understand them without knowing something of those times. Initially, the Israelites saw their God as a tribal God, who helped them win battles. If they won, God was pleased with them. If they lost, they had not pleased God in some way, or the other God was more powerful. When they were taken by the Babylonians into captivity, they thought their God had been left behind in the promised land. Gradually the idea came into being, through the prophets, that this was no tribal God, but the one and only God. And the nature of God was gradually being realised as well. Far from being a tribal, jealous, wrathful God, he was compassionate, kind, patient. When Jesus came on the scene, he brought to fruition this gradual dawning of God as a loving parent with whom we can become One, and showed how to lead a God-filled life of compassion and self-emptying, beholden to no one but God. This eventually led to his death, as that sort of life was a huge challenge to the status quo of the religious hierarchy.

Some Interesting Facts

Understanding the different styles of writing and the difficulty with the translation of some words can give us insight into the diversity of the Bible and what we lose in translation. Here are two examples.

Acrostic Psalms

Psalm 119 is a lengthy and carefully constructed poem – a particular type of poem called an acrostic. An acrostic is a poem where each line, or each section, begins with successive letters of the alphabet. In the Hebrew alphabet, there are 22 letters and there is one section for each letter. The first section, verses 1–8, is the "aleph" section, or A. The second section begins with the Hebrew letter "beth", the equivalent of our letter B, and so on. Each section has eight lines. Every line within any one section begins with the same Hebrew letter. Also, there are eight Hebrew words for law. Within each section, all the eight Hebrew words for "law" occur. Why the writer did it like this, I don't know – I think it's what writers do! It's a highly structured, carefully written poem. The trouble is, we lose all of that when it is translated into English. A similar technique is

used in Lamentations 3 and several other places in the Hebrew
Scriptures.

YHWH

Throughout most English translations of the Hebrew Scriptures,
the word "LORD" in capital letters is actually a representation
(or misrepresentation) of the four letters "YHWH" (called the
tetragrammaton). It stems from the encounter of Moses with
the burning bush, from which God speaks, telling him to go to
Pharaoh and ask him to set the Israelites free. Ancient Hebrew
did not have vowels, only consonants, and it was all written in
capital letters with no spaces, so you can see translation is a bit
tricky! YHWH can be translated as meaning "I am who I am", or
"I will be who I will be", or even "I cause to be what I cause to
be", or just "I am Being." In the reading of the Hebrew Scriptures
during Jewish worship, "I AM" was a constant reminder to the
Jews of the name of God. In most English translations, we find
YHWH translated as LORD (in capital letters). Why should this
be so? Bruce Metzger, in the introduction to the New Revised
Standard Version of the Bible, explains that the original Hebrew
had only consonants and no vowel sounds indicated. These
were added by Jewish scholars called the Masoretes between
the seventh and tenth centuries CE. By the time the Masoretes
added vowel sounds to the text, the name of God had come to be
considered too sacred to be pronounced, so they attached vowel
signs indicating that in its place should be read the Hebrew
word *Adonai*, meaning "Lord". Unfortunately, this practice was
adopted by most English translators. "LORD" gives a title to
God that has all sorts of overtones of power, dominance and
control and loses the idea that we are all interconnected within
this Being.

We also lose the connection with Jesus' statements as recorded
in John's gospel. When Jesus said, "Before Abraham was born, I
am," or "I am the way, the truth and the life," it would be heard

by the Jews as more like "Before Abraham was born, I was in God", and "God in me is the way, the truth and the life." Jesus was implying that his identity was located in the consciousness of God within him. Jesus was a fully human being, not more human than you and I, so this can be seen as way of saying that the God of all is present in everyone, and the potential is there for anyone to become fully divine if they can open to that God presence and live their lives from it. "I AM" referred to the eternal Logos or Word of God, the Universal Christ who was with the Father before the foundation of the world, who holds everything in being, and not the human Jesus born of Mary. Because most English translations use LORD instead of YHWH or I AM, we have totally lost that association in the Western Church with the "I am" statements that Jesus made.

The Nativity Stories

Understanding the writing conventions of the time means we can respect the texts, yet also look for the deeper meanings. What is the author trying to imply? The nativity story is a case in point. I should say stories, as there are two different ones in Matthew and Luke, but they are inevitably conflated into one whole as the "Christmas Nativity". On the surface, it's a story of miracles – we find the virgin birth, angels singing in the sky, a moving star in the heavens and a series of strange events. But at another level it has deeper meanings. So what are those deeper meanings?

Some Christians understand the nativity as a literally true story that the two gospel writers based on actual eyewitness accounts, despite the anomalies and differences between Matthew's version and Luke's. Or it can be seen as an allegorical or metaphorical story which sets the scene for the main story to come. The gospel writers wanted everyone to know about what Jesus said and did in his years of ministry, and so the nativity story points ahead to the significant truths of the momentous events that happen during the ministry years of Jesus the Messiah, and in his death and resurrection. It builds up, enhances and complements the rest of the gospel. It was an accepted way of "heralding" the story of the man which was to follow, and in its own time would not necessarily have been understood as literally true, but recognised as a linguistic technique used by writers.

Those outside Christianity often class the nativity as a fairy story. It is not, it is a story of great significance in the gospels, whether you see it as factual or allegorical. It weaves together elements of expectation, anticipation and hope from the Hebrew Scriptures and joins them to the New Testament. It's like that old native American storyteller says as he begins his tribe's story of creation "I don't know whether it happened this way or not, but I know this story is true." Or a Catholic priest who once said "The Bible is true – and some of it happened." There's little point arguing about "whether it happened exactly this way or not", because the story really is pointing to the greater truths and deeper meanings.

- The story of Jesus being conceived by the Spirit of God affirms that what happened in Jesus was of God. This man that the rest of the gospel is about, was totally God-filled, at-one with God.
- The angels filling the sky with light and the special star suggest light in the darkness, breaking into our reality, a special gift to the world. Light in the darkness is a powerful symbol.
- The story of the shepherds shows that there is a special place for the marginalised, the poor, the disadvantaged. That is exactly who Jesus had time for and is a theme of Luke's gospel.
- The song of the angels declares Jesus as Lord and Saviour – and not the Roman emperor, who used those titles for

himself. The gospel writers challenged Roman rule in subtle and not so subtle ways.

- The story of the foreign wise magi (astrologers) from lands afar, who have always been portrayed as men, affirms that Jesus is the light for all peoples, not just the Jews.
- The story of Herod killing the innocents shows how important this birth was – even kings were threatened by it. (That bit is not often included in retellings of the nativity, a bit too gruesome.)

The gifts of the wise magi signify different things as well. Gold carries obvious significance. It's precious and worthy across all cultures and times. It's a gift fit for royalty. It says about the Christ child, he will be a king. Frankincense was burned in the ancient world, as a symbol of prayers being carried to heaven. Its use as incense illustrates his future priestly role. It is still used in churches today as a symbol of prayers rising to God. Myrrh's most notable use was that of an embalming material, used in Egyptian mummies. As an embalming ointment it was a symbol of death. Myrrh was one of the burial spices used on Jesus (John 19:39).

This was all part of the heralding of the rest of the story, and not to be seen as literally true events. Read metaphorically, the nativity story means all of this and more. And it means it independently of whether we see it as a factual story or not. Arguing about whether these things actually happened or not distracts from their deeper meaning and loses something of their significance. To insert some dramatic events to do with the person's birth was a common way of introducing a story about someone's life in those days. I don't believe they did happen, but that doesn't detract from the Christmas story for me. It is a mythological presentation of the "birth of Christ in the heart", the awakening, that has to happen in every human soul at some stage, to the path back home to the Divine Source. The Christ-consciousness in each of us is born in humility, in letting go of self-centredness and in opening to love.

Creation Stories and Science

Another area of interpretation is the beginning of the Book of Genesis, the story of Creation. In my view, there is a way of looking at this which is consistent with both modern science and Christianity. I used to be a science teacher. At school, I was always wanting to know how things worked, so I studied the sciences, especially physics, because it asks just that question – how does it all work? And later, as I was teaching science, I became interested in spirituality, and I wanted to know the answers to the same question – how does it all work? I have found over the years that a lot of the standard theological answers just don't cut it for me, or don't hang together properly with the world as we know it now, and interestingly, I have turned back to science for some deeper thoughts.

The book of Genesis gives us the story of the seven days of creation. In Hebrew numerology, seven is the number of perfection (see Chapter 6 on numerology). Coming from about 3000 years ago, it is an epic story of beginnings, framed in the understanding of the time. Our understanding is now that there was a big bang some 13.7 billion years ago, an enormous explosion which brought light energy and matter into being from some other realm of existence. "Let there be light" was indeed the beginning of creation. In that moment of creation, space and time were formed, electromagnetism was formed, gravity was formed and all the rules by which the universe operates were formed – the laws of physics. And from that point, everything has evolved according to those laws of physics.

But what was it that formed all these foundational axioms? It's the age-old question, who created the creator? And why should the universe exist according to those laws? Many scientists have calculated that if those laws of physics were different by the tiniest, most miniscule fraction, then stars would not have formed, planets would not exist, and the universe would be completely different. So why are those laws so finely and precisely balanced to bring forth life? That's one thing which is perplexing scientists these days, and has been since the early days of modern science, back in the 1920s.

One of the perplexing things about quantum theory is that some form of consciousness that can observe has to exist in order for the particles of matter to come into being. It sounds totally weird, but basically, the quantum insight says that if there is no consciousness in the beginning, then particles would never have come into existence and the material world that we live in and are part of could not exist. There has to be a universal "mind" at the beginning of creation. Consciousness is the underlying reality of everything, the matrix in which everything is held.

Max Planck was one of the great scientists of all time. In his later years, he said:

> As a man who has devoted his whole life to the most clear-headed science, to the study of matter, I can tell you, as the result of my research about atoms, this much: There is no matter as such! All matter originates and exists only by virtue of a force.... We must assume behind this force the existence of a conscious and intelligent mind. This mind is the matrix of all matter.

So consciousness, from a quantum physics perspective is seen as a divine matrix, the ground of being, in which all material possibilities are held in potential. Consciousness as the "ground of being" sounds like another way of talking about God. The Christian understanding is that God holds everything in being, is infinitely creative, and sustains all. We can read of this in the New Testament, referring to the Christ, or Logos (word) of God.

In the beginning was the Word, and the Word was with God, and the Word was God. He was in the beginning with God. All things came into being through him, and without him not one thing came into being. (John 1:1–3a)

This is the creative principle, the divine Word being breathed out into the universe and hence everything came into being from God, the ground of being. Without that divine consciousness, nothing material would exist, because, according to the laws of quantum physics, in order for any matter to exist, there has to be a consciousness observing it.

All things were created by him and for him. He is before all things, and in him all things hold together. (Colossians 1:16–17)

The Son is the radiance of God's glory and the exact representation of his being, sustaining all things by his powerful word. (Hebrews 1:3)

Both these verses tell us that God sustains everything in being, including space and time. So the theological concept that God sustains all things in being dovetails neatly with quantum physics that consciousness is the ground of being. We can begin to think of God as the immense consciousness which holds the universe in being, which is called the Godhead in Christianity. This is God as the creative principle, bringing the universe into existence and sustaining it "by his mighty word", which is his energy poured out through his consciousness.

Where does that leave us as individuals? As the Bible puts it, "God's Spirit lives in you". We are the temple of the Holy Spirit, or the Holy Breath (the same word in both Hebrew and Greek). God breathes us into existence, through, of course, a process of evolution. In every human being, there is a spark of God-consciousness, the God within that is a real part of us, because we only exist within that consciousness. It could be said we are part of God. But only in as much as a single drop of water could be said to be part of the same water as in the seas, the air and the clouds, the whole biosphere. We as individuals cannot fathom the limitlessness of the consciousness that sustains the whole of creation in being, that works through all sentient beings throughout the universe. In that sense, we are not God. So we have a paradox – we are both God and not God. We are both part of the wave field of God-consciousness, yet we are also individual beings – which is the heart of the quantum paradox!

Opening ourselves up to this divine drop of God-consciousness happens through religious experience, worship, meditation, contemplative prayer, mystical experience, and at moments of heightened reality. In these experiences, our own individual ego-selves are put aside and we become aware of the sea of God-consciousness of which we are a miniscule drop. The ultimate religious experience is of oneness with God. Anyone who has had a mystical experience of union with God will see all this as already known and accepted. The big difference is that science is now slowly and reluctantly beginning to come around to the viewpoint that spiritual people have held for millennia! There is only one, and we are part of it. Jesus used his own shorthand for this, talking about the kingdom of God, a new way of being. This was the good news he came to proclaim, that the kingdom of God was near.

Jesus said, "The time has come! God's kingdom will soon be here. Turn back to God and believe the good news!" (Mark 1:15 CEV)

Being "in the kingdom" means an awareness of being held in the consciousness of God, connected to the Ground of Being. The revelation that came with Christ Jesus moved us on so that we can see that this God, in whom we live and move and have our being, is also the God of love, and this consciousness which holds us all in being is a compassionate, loving consciousness.

Some of the words from John's gospel begin to make much more sense in the light of understanding the kingdom as being at one with the consciousness of God. Jesus said:

I and the Father are one. John 10:30
I am in my Father, and you in me and I in you. John 14:20
He who abides in me, and I in him, will bear much fruit. John 15:5
They may be one as we are one. I in them and you in me. May they
be brought to complete unity. John17:22–23

These, and many more, all point to Jesus' understanding and experience of this divine, unitive consciousness. My view is that he was fulfilling the human potential to be one with God, and in doing so, he operated from a higher consciousness than the rest of humanity at the time.

The message of Christianity is that, as we turn to God, as we move into an awareness of the divine presence in the depths of our being, so we grow to be more compassionate people, so we change, we are transformed into people of the kingdom of God, the image of Christ, living in the field of loving consciousness. In this way, we are bringing the whole world a little closer to living out the kingdom vision that so inspired Jesus. The words of Jesus are, "Seek first his kingdom and his righteousness" or, to expand that a little in my own words: Put first in your life the search for God's presence within you, to find the holiness of heart and purity of life which is your true home in the divine consciousness.

Summary

Interpretation is not easy. The meaning of ancient words can be lost or has changed drastically. We see this in our own lifetimes. Fifty years ago, to say "You are wicked!" meant you are accusing someone of being evil. Say it now, and you are telling someone they are "cool". Words change their meanings. Cultures and morals change as consciousness evolves. What is abhorrent now was considered acceptable years ago. The worst of the Spanish Inquisition was only five hundred years ago, approximately fifteen generations in our past, and thousands were killed as heretics. It wasn't finally officially abolished until 1834 by Royal Spanish Decree. Moral standards change. Treating the Bible as infallible and inerrant makes a nonsense of common sense. We have to use our own discernment and highest levels of perception to interpret texts for today, not just accept what was said about them with a medieval mentality. Prayerful reflection on the meaning of texts for today is essential.

Questions for Reflection

1. How can we understand the Bible as "the Word of God?"
2. In the Anglican and Roman Catholic Church, after the Bible is read, the words "This is the word of the Lord. Thanks be to God" are often used. Do you have any problem with that?
3. How has your own understanding of the Bible changed over the years?
4. What passages in the Bible do you find particularly problematic, and why?

Further Study Resources

It is worth reading the introduction in the New International Version of the Bible, or the New Revised Standard Version, to get an idea of the complicated nature of translating ancient texts into English.

Rohr, Richard, 2008. *Things Hidden: Scripture as Spirituality.* Cincinnati OH: St Anthony Messenger Press

Chapter 5

Reinterpretations

All languages have their own idiosyncrasies and colloquialisms, English more than most. Consider the expressions for not feeling very well. You can be "under the weather", which does not mean it is raining, or "below par" when you are not playing golf. Or in Scotland you could be feeling "peely-wally!" Those who know the meaning have lived with the phrases, but coming afresh to them, they don't make much sense. Some words have many different meanings. For example, "The archer wore his necktie in a bow and carried his bow to bow to the king." Three different uses of the same word in one sentence, two of them with the same pronunciation! The same word can have many meanings. Also complicating matters is that the words of Jesus were spoken in his native language of Aramaic, but written down later in Greek, and then translated to English, sometimes via Latin. Aramaic is a more poetic language in which words have many shades of meaning. Translating to Greek means having to choose one word from amongst several possibilities. Plenty of room for error and mistranslations!

Re-Languaging Spirit and Spirituality

Language is always a problem in trying to communicate spiritual concepts and ideas because we are dealing with experiences of the divine that can be interpreted differently by every individual. In any system of thought or cultural milieu, a vocabulary develops to communicate in that sphere, whether it is medical terminology, the world of music, the legal system, education or religious thought. Each develops its own "jargon". All of the major religious and spiritual viewpoints have their own language.

Spirituality is about the human experience of the Divine. We then try to put into words this numinous experience. The experience itself can be of several types:

- Being taken up in a feeling and knowing of such awe and wonder that we know we are one with everything, and are held in love. It is the mystical experience of being at one with the Divine, unity awareness, oneness, often called non-duality.
- Receiving or becoming a channel for messages from subtle realms by visions or voices.
- Intuitive understanding coming from subtle realms, which we might call inspiration.

These are normal human experiences, although not felt by everyone, but experienced by some for millennia, and something possible for anyone to have, given the right conditions, the right psychological and spiritual development. The experiences are then interpreted in the understanding of the time and culture and context of that person. So the articulation of these experiences takes on the *clothing* of the religious and moral system of the time. The problem is, we can mistake the clothing for the inner human spiritual experience, which leads us to imagine differences where actually none exist. Language is tricky. Religious practices are different, but surely the human felt-experience of the Divine is actually the same across all faiths.

The Liturgy Problem

The language of liturgical Christianity in the West tends to come from the biblical and medieval worldview of a three-tiered universe. In this model, humanity has its fragile existence in the middle layer of the firmament, the earth, and above us are the heavens, where God and the angels live. Below us is hell or the underworld. We are all aware that the universe is not like that, but much of the language still reinforces it, as in the Lord's Prayer. "Our Father, who art in heaven" tells us that God is still "up in heaven", distinct from us. The old language was about separateness, exclusivity, patriarchy, the almighty, omniscient nature of God, Lord and Master, and is based on tribal thinking. This mode of thought defines who is "in" and who is "out". It sees humanity as fallen, not inherently divine. It is also about divine transaction, not human transformation. Interestingly, Eastern Orthodoxy has always retained the concept that humanity can become divinised, which is the final goal of transformation.

But the new spirituality is developing its own language, partly scientific, partly spiritual. The core of it seems to be that we are all part of the One Consciousness which holds everything in being, permeates everything and is the One Life "in which we live and move and have our being," to quote St Paul. There is a growing awareness that we are all one interconnected whole, not just with the rest of humanity, but with the whole of the biosphere. As Dr. Jude Currivan says in her book *The Cosmic Hologram*, "Consciousness isn't just something we have, it's what we and the whole world **are**."

A New Language

So the language that is emerging around this new spiritual story includes these sorts of words – oneness, interconnectedness, consciousness, source, Gaia, energies, non-duality, transcendence, transformation, awakening, awareness, evolution, initiation, gender equality, inclusion, ecology, interdependence, unity. But there are strong crossover points with traditional faiths, connecting words between the different views. The connecting words are mostly *qualities*, such as love, respect, honour, kindness, goodness, peacefulness, will-to-good, heart, compassion. Dr Neil Douglas-Klotz has done some very good work in looking at the Aramaic words that Jesus would have spoken, but which were written down in Greek. As mentioned, Aramaic is a much more poetic language with many more shades of meaning, which his work expands into. Here is a worked example of the Lord's Prayer freely translated from the shades of meaning in the Aramaic that Jesus spoke, based on the ideas of Neil Douglas-Klotz in *Prayers of the Cosmos*.

Traditional Version

Our Father who art in heaven, hallowed be thy name.
Thy kingdom come, thy will be done, on earth as it is in
    heaven.
Give us this day our daily bread,
    and forgive us our trespasses as we forgive those who
    trespass against us.
And lead us not into temptation, but deliver us from evil.
For thine is the kingdom and the power and the glory,
    forever and ever.
Amen.

Free translation from Aramaic:

O Breath of Life, flowing in all creation, may the light of
    your presence fill the universe.
Your way of being come, your desire be done, in this and all
    realms of existence.
Bring forth the nourishment and insight we need for this
    day.
May forgiveness of self and others be our lived reality.
Liberate us from all things that bind us and deliver us from
    unhealthiness.
For you are abundant life, creative unity and glorious
    harmony,
through all time and beyond.
So be it.

In my previous book, *Blue Sky God: The Evolution of Science and Christianity*, I tried rewriting several of the traditional prayers of the Anglican Church, putting them into twenty-first-century language. Here are two examples, with the traditional wording followed by my own rendering:

The Collect for Purity

Almighty God, to whom all hearts are open, all desires known, and from whom no secrets are hidden: cleanse the thoughts of our hearts by the inspiration of your Holy Spirit, that we may perfectly love you, and worthily magnify your holy name; through Christ our Lord. Amen.

God of all compassion, whose presence within sees our heart's desires and hidden secrets: let your energy and light flow, so that we may know your breath of life in our inner beings, and show heartfelt praise in our lives, as did Jesus the Christ. Let it be so.

The Confession

Almighty God, our heavenly Father, we have sinned
    against you and against our fellow men, in thought and
    word and deed, through negligence, through weakness,
    through our own deliberate fault.
We are truly sorry, and repent of all our sins.
For the sake of your Son Jesus Christ, who died for us,
    forgive us all that is past;
    and grant that we may serve you in newness of life, to the
    glory of your name. Amen.

God of all Creation, in whom we live and move and have
    our being,
    we acknowledge our separation from you within, our
    self-centredness

and hardness of heart towards others and ourselves.

We are truly sorry, and ask that you would help us to move
beyond our smallness into the heart of your loving,
expansive presence.

May we be remade in the image of Jesus the Christ, the
divine human,
that we may know fullness of life in the energy of your
love. Let it be so.

We can be creative; it is why we have minds! Creativity allows
modern expressions of timeless truths, which can hopefully
reach new generations to inspire and encourage young minds in
spiritual exploration. The traditional words are often comforting
to those who have used them all their lives, but for those who are
not familiar with them, they can create a blockage to progressing
on a spiritual path.

The Message of Jesus

Interpreting ancient words to get the true meaning from them
is especially important when we consider what Jesus said. What
was the core of his message? What did he preach? What did he
demonstrate? Let's look at the message in Matthew's gospel:

*From that time Jesus began to proclaim [preach], "Repent, for the
kingdom of heaven has come near." (Matthew 4:17)*

When it says Jesus began to preach or proclaim, the word had a
slightly different meaning from what it has now. Today we can
use it in a derogatory sense: "Don't you preach at me!" Or do we
associate it with the idea that preaching is like a sleeping pill,
time to nod off or daydream. In Greek the word was *kerussein*
which is the word for a herald's proclamation from a king – the
herald brought a message of authority; it wasn't his message,
it was the king's. People sat up and paid attention. The herald

brought a message from a source, an authority beyond himself. It is saying that Jesus' message came from a source beyond himself, from God, the one he called "Father".

Matthew's gospel takes a while building up to what he has to tell us about Jesus' message. He has a long and comprehensive prologue to the good news. He starts his prologue with a genealogy to show that Jesus is descended from Abraham, then he goes on to the nativity story and the flight to Egypt. Then he jumps to John the Baptist and Jesus' baptism and anointing by the Holy Spirit, followed by the temptations in the desert. Having built up the expectations of the reader with all this, he then gets down to the meat of what he has to tell us, which is Jesus' message, his preaching, his parables, his way of living, his compassion, his healing.

"Repent, for the kingdom of God is near" was Jesus' first declaration. Repent does **not** mean "Say you are sorry!" It means literally "Change your mind". Change your worldview. Have a paradigm shift. Start looking at things in a different way, God's way. Turn around and lift your eyes from material things to look to spiritual things. Build your treasures in heaven. Move your centre of consciousness to a higher place. In St Paul's words, "Be transformed by the renewing of your mind" (Romans 12:2). We are called to shift up a few gears to a finer vibrational level of consciousness.

"The kingdom of God is near." Jesus' teaching, his good news, was all about the kingdom of God, by which he meant the highest and best and most compassionate of values, attitudes and morals by which we can live, coming from the purest and finest vibrational source. After this passage, Matthew sets out the teaching in the Sermon on the Mount – the Beatitudes, about being salt and light in the world, about relationships, about loving others, even your enemy, giving, trusting, not judging, praying, storing up treasures in heaven and so on. This is the manifesto for living in the kingdom of God. Jesus wasn't talking about getting a reward in heaven when you die, he was talking about living in the best way now. It was his manifesto for living in this life, not for getting to heaven after death. This was the kingdom, the reign of God, the way that Jesus wanted everyone to live now.

A New Way

Jesus went throughout Galilee, teaching in their synagogues and proclaiming the good news of the kingdom and curing every disease and every sickness among the people. (Matthew 4:23)

This new way of living is for the highest good of the human race. If we can overcome our base nature, overcome the greed, pride and territorial nature that causes arguments, disputes, and wars, and if we can show compassion to all our fellow human beings and the whole created order, then we shall be fulfilling the potential of the human race, we shall be rising to a new level of spiritual awareness, a new consciousness that is in tune with God, an anointed, Christed humanity.

Saved or Healed?

The good news that Jesus brought was intimately connected with healing and wholeness. When I look up the verb *to save* in the Greek, I find that there are two words – *sozo*, meaning deliverance from danger, suffering etc., and *diasozo*, meaning to bring safely through. But when I look up the verb *to heal*, I find the same two words.

- *Sozo* means both to save, and to heal, to make whole.
- *Diasozo*, means both to bring safely through, and to heal completely.

So modern Bible translators, in doing their work translating from Greek to English, have to decide, from the context, whether to translate the words as save or heal. And they are inevitably influenced by 1500 years of the erroneous idea that Jesus was always talking about saving from sin, eternal salvation, whether you are going to get to heaven or not. The Church has constantly been talking about that, but Jesus wasn't. Most of the time, he was talking about making people whole, healing sickness and disease. He was talking about healing from wrong ways of thinking, wrong attitudes, bad experiences, psychological hurts and traumas. The church in its early doctrine put it all into an eternal salvation context, "If you believe in Jesus, you will have eternal life in heaven," but that was not the intention of Jesus. Eternal salvation is the outer meaning given by the Church, not the inner transformative meaning of Jesus. It is the exoteric sense not the esoteric, Jesus "saves" means that following Jesus brings wholeness and purpose in this life, this existence, this vale of soul-making. Jesus never said "Worship me", but he did say repeatedly, "Follow me".

The Woman of Ill-Repute

As an example of mistranslation, take the story in Luke 7:36–50 of the woman who comes to the meal that Jesus took part in at the home of Simon the Pharisee. This woman of "ill-repute" turned up and, as Jesus reclined at the table, she anointed his feet with oil and her own tears, wiping them with her hair, kissing his feet. We are told several times she is a sinner. Jesus tells her that her sins are forgiven. Then he says to her "Your faith has saved you: go in peace." All the English translations use the same English word; your faith has *saved* you. In the Greek, the word is *sozo*, with the sense of being delivered from, protected from, healed and made whole. Jesus himself would have been speaking in Hebrew or Aramaic, closely related languages. In Hebrew, the word is *yesha*, meaning to be free, in a wide or roomy space, carrying the sense of being freed from confinement, constriction and limitation.

Now I think Jesus was far more likely to have said to the woman "Your faith has *healed* you, go in peace." That is the meaning of "saved" within the Judaic world at the time. That is what the woman needed, healing from all the past hurt, the emotional damage that had led her into prostitution, if that was indeed her sin. She wasn't looking for a promise that she would be with God after death, she was seeking emotional relief from the torment of now. She wanted to be more whole, and that is what Jesus did for her – he healed her of the emotional scars and damage that had been crippling her for years, he set her free, released her from captivity, and guided her into the kingdom of God in the here and now.

It pains me to think that the words of Jesus have been slanted far more to thinking about eternal salvation than about healing and wholeness in the here and now – because that is what the world needs to hear, that there is a better way of living, a better way of life that can bring freedom and healing and wholeness to the human race. It would be a real epiphany if the whole world woke up to that! It is not tied exclusively to Jesus, but is available to anyone who chooses to follow the same path of compassion and self-renunciation that he did, which is there in most other faiths. Humanity certainly needs to find a better way of living and relating, and this is gradually dawning on many around the world today. As I write, we are in the midst of the Covid-19 pandemic, and the message that there can be a better way for humanity is emerging from many quarters. Different interpretations of the ancient early Christian texts can help bring out a whole new meaning of the words of Jesus.

The Jesus Way

So I believe Jesus proclaimed the message of the good news of the kingdom, and it was good news because it addressed issues and needs in the immediate world. He was not aiming to start a new religion, he was reinvigorating the old one, getting back to the basics, the life-giving virtues and qualities that are inherent in all good spiritual teaching. He wasn't asking to be worshipped, he was wanting us to be like him, to follow him. He set out, in his teaching and demonstrated in his life, a way of being that was for all to follow. It revolved around being changed in our inner attitudes towards others, to love one another, lifting ourselves from the lower self-centred nature to a higher state. We then begin to grow in compassion for all, turning to the One Divine Inner Presence in prayer for strength, seeking the best for everyone, mending broken lives, and bringing light into the world now. When the world seems dark, we are all invited to follow Jesus in walking into the light, to pray for the healing of the nations and for the kingdom of God to come in our time.

This is a major step in the evolution of humanity. The Wisdom teachings call it an initiation that the human race is going through, an awakening to new levels of being. There are all sorts of ingrained attitudes and patterns of thought that have to be overcome, burnt up, in order for us to move on. Many of these old patterns are being highlighted at this time in politics, economics, health-care, religion, education and other areas of human endeavour. In bringing them to the fore, we see what we do not want and can then work for change. The teachings emphasise that this is all divinely guided via the energetic emanations from higher planes of divinity, which Christianity would categorise as the work of the Holy Spirit.

Summary

Terminology can be a barrier unless we understand that all spiritual experience is ultimately beyond words and descriptions, and we struggle with crossing over from the set of words of one view to the differing set of another way of explaining the same types of experience. A kiss can be defined as "to touch or caress with the lips as a sign of love, sexual desire, or greeting." Or it can be defined as "The anatomical juxtaposition of two orbicularis oris muscles in a state of contraction." The same experience, but the explanations come from different spheres of understanding.

In further complication, many words have gained meanings that are now different from when they were first used. A fresh look, not holding to accepted norms and habits of the past, could revolutionise some biblical translations. It takes boldness, or is it desperation, to challenge the authority figures within church contexts, but some are doing just that.

Questions for Reflection

1. What words or phrases do you struggle with in Church liturgy? Try looking them up online to dig deeper into the theological understanding.
2. How can we be change instigators in local churches? Can we research and offer new liturgical resources? Can we introduce new ideas within small groups?

Further Study Resources

Borg, Marcus, 2011. *Speaking Christian: Recovering the Lost Meaning of Christian Words.* London: SPCK

Douglas-Klotz, N.,1994. *Prayers of the Cosmos: Meditations on the Aramaic Words of Jesus.* New York: HarperCollins Publishers

Douglas-Klotz, N., 1999. *The Hidden Gospel.* Wheaton (IL): Quest Books

Henson, J., 2004. *Good as New: A Radical Retelling of the Scriptures.* Winchester UK: O Books

Henson, J., 2010. *Wide Awake Worship: Hymns and Prayers Renewed for the 21st Century.* Winchester UK: O Books

Hodson, Geoffrey, 1993. *Hidden Wisdom in the Holy Bible, Vol. 1.* Wheaton IL: Quest Books

MacGregor, Don, 2012. *Blue Sky God: The Evolution of Science and Christianity.* Alresford UK: Circle Books – (particularly chapters 6, 7 and 9)

Taussig, Hal (ed.), 2015. *A New New Testament: A Bible for the 21st Century.* New York: Houghton Mifflin Harcourt Publishing Co

Chapter 6

Why Numbers Matter

Threes

Anyone who writes or speaks publically will know about alliteration, and that it works best in threes. Always alliterate artfully. Emphasis in speech simply *works* in threes, we emphasise, we underline, we restate. There's a wholeness to the meaning each time we use a three-fold repetition. It is somehow the whole thing, rounded, complete. All preachers know that the three-point sermon works best. Education uses the term "the three Rs", representing a complete basic education. Three cheers make one whole congratulation.

You might have been there, done that, got the T-shirt. Or you swallowed it all, hook, line and sinker. Or you are a busy person – things to do, places to go, people to see. Or you have a chance to relax – eat, drink and be merry. We use threes all the time!

In the natural world, there are three phases of matter: solids, liquids, and gases (I know some class "plasma" as a fourth, but it is really a sub-set of gases). There are three realms in nature: animal, vegetable, and mineral. We live in a 3-D universe with three basic dimensions: length, width, height. There are three primary colours: yellow, red, and blue, from which you can make all others. I could go on!

Three seems to be a perfect number. Complete, containing everything. In liturgy, threes appear often:

- Christ has died, Christ is risen, Christ will come again – it contains the whole theology of Christ.
- Holy, holy, holy, Lord God almighty – meaning perfectly holy, set apart (not that I agree that God is set apart!).
- Lord have mercy, Christ have mercy, Lord have mercy –

God offers complete forgiveness.

Why should this "threeness" be so? We simply *feel* it to be a completeness, a wholeness, like it is built into the fabric of reality. We just *know* it works. Biblical writers went far further than this, using numbers to signify many different qualities, which is rarely brought out in church teaching. Many of the scriptures contain numerically coded messages. So what are the significant numbers? Here's a short guide to the major ones.

One

One indicates unity, divinity, and wholeness, as exemplified by God.

> *There is one body and one Spirit, just as you were called to the one hope of your calling, one Lord, one faith, one baptism, one God and Father of all, who is above all and through all and in all. (Ephesians 4:4–6)*

Three

As we've seen above, three most often stands for wholeness, completeness and perfection. It describes the whole thing, lock, stock and barrel. The Holy Trinity is a foundational understanding of the Three-in-One God, Father, Son and Holy Spirit. Also, as Paul says in his wonderful passage about love in 1 Corinthians 13, the most important and abiding graces are three, but only one is the best:

> *And now faith, hope, and love abide, these three; and the greatest of these is love. (1 Corinthians 13:13)*

There are many more examples:

- the three temptations of Christ (Matthew 4:1–11)

- the three denials of Peter (John 18:13–27)
- three times a year, the Israelites were commanded to hold a festival for God (Exodus 23:14–19)
- prayer was urged three times daily (see Daniel 6:10 and Psalm 55:17)
- three-year-old animals were divinely requested for special sacrifices (Genesis 15:9)

Four

Four signifies a sense of the totality of God's work. It is associated with creation, the earth's four seasons, the four primary lunar phases, four classical elements of earth, water, air and fire. The Book of Numbers just happens to be the fourth book of the Bible and four occurs frequently in the Book of Revelation.

Around the throne, and on each side of the throne, are four living creatures, full of eyes in front and behind. (Revelation 4:6)

After this I saw four angels standing at the four corners of the earth, holding back the four winds of the earth so that no wind could blow on earth or sea or against any tree. (Revelation 7:1)

In Judaism, the Passover Seder meal is particularly structured around fours: the Four Questions, the Four Sons, and four cups of wine.

Six

Six indicates imperfection. It is often associated with humanity, created on the sixth day, and riddled with imperfections and failings, but, even so, close to seven, representing Godly perfection. The number of the beast in Revelation 13:18 is 666, signifying everything that falls short of perfection.

Seven

Seven signifies, more than any other, the totality of perfection and completeness. The Bible is replete with things grouped in sevens.

- There are seven days of creation and God blessed the seventh day and made it holy (Genesis 2:3).
- Noah was instructed to take seven pairs of all clean animals onboard the ark (Genesis 7:2).
- There are seven colours in the rainbow, the symbol of the new covenant with Noah.
- The Pharaoh's dream was of seven fat cows, followed by seven thin cows and there were seven years of plenty followed by seven years of famine.
- The menorah in the Temple has seven branches with seven candles.
- Jesus said that forgiveness is to be offered not just seven times, but seventy times seven times, or endlessly (Matthew 18:21–22).
- In the Book of Revelation, there are multiple examples including: seven churches (Revelation 2:1–3:22), seven bowls (Revelation 15:5–16:21), seven seals (Revelation 5:1–8:1), seven trumpets (Revelation 8:2–11:18), seven thunders (Revelation 10:3–4), seven spirits (Revelation 1:4), seven stars (Revelation 1:20), and seven lampstands (Revelation 1:20). The lamb has seven eyes and seven horns (Revelation 5:6). The dragon has seven heads and seven diadems (Revelation 12:3), and the beast from the sea has seven heads (Revelation 13:1; 17:3).
- There is a total of three hundred and eighty-three verses in the Bible that use seven as the number of items.
- In addition, there are seven official sacraments in the Roman Catholic and Orthodox churches.

Eight

Eight signifies new beginnings, new life, resurrection. Examples include:

- There were eight people on Noah's Ark (Gen 7:7, 2 Peter 2:5) to make a new start.
- Circumcision happened on the eighth day, confirming new life and signifying the new covenant (Gen 17:12).
- Jesus was crucified on the sixth day (imperfection), rested in the tomb on the Sabbath, the seventh day (completion), and rose from the dead on the eighth day (resurrection, the new start).

Twelve

Twelve represents the completion of God's purpose, the optimal number to carry out the Divine Plan.

- Jacob had twelve sons, which became the twelve tribes of Israel.
- There were twelve chosen apostles (Matthew 10:2, Revelation 21:14).
- The dedication offering for the altar in the tabernacle, its point of completion for use, contained twelve of everything (Numbers 7:84–87). There were twelve silver plates, twelve silver sprinkling bowls and twelve gold dishes. The burnt offering was twelve young bulls, twelve rams and twelve male lambs a year old. Twelve male goats were used for the sin offering.
- Twelve features hugely in Revelation. The woman's crown has twelve stars (Revelation 12:1). The new Jerusalem in Revelation 21–22 is completely designed with twelves. There are twelve angels at the twelve gates, and the names of the twelve tribes are inscribed on the gates. The twelve foundations of the city wall have the twelve names of the

apostles and the wall is twelve squared, equalling 144 cubits. Twelve jewels adorn the foundations; and it has twelve gates. The tree of life has twelve kinds of fruit for the healing of the nations. The new Jerusalem measures 12,000 stadia on each side (Revelation 21:16), forming a perfect cube and dwelling place for all God's people.

- Twelve is lengthened to 144,000 (12 x 12 x 1,000) in Revelation 7:4; 14:1,3 and indicates the totality of the redeemed people of God, which I think means all shall be brought into the presence of God.

Forty

The number forty is also a recurring Bible theme and represents trials and testing. It first appears in the story of the flood (Genesis 7:4) when it rained for forty days and forty nights. Moses was associated with forty several times: he was forty years old when he was exiled from Egypt for killing an Egyptian, he spent forty years as a shepherd before returning with the plagues to eventually lead the Hebrews out of captivity. He was forty days on Mount Sinai, and with the rest of the Israelites he wandered in the desert for forty years before reaching the promised land. Later on, Goliath challenged the Israelites for forty days before David killed him. King David ruled for forty years. In the New Testament, Jesus was tempted by Satan in the desert for forty days. Jesus also remained in Jerusalem and Galilee for forty days before his ascension.

Something Fishy

Numbers really mattered to the writers of scripture. When the New Testament was written, the early Christians found nothing strange in involving numerology in their expressions of faith. There is one passage which always puzzled me until I started looking into numerology – the story in John's gospel of the miraculous catch of fish, where a very exact number is specified

– 153 fish were caught. Why was the author so specific?

There was, at the time, a philosophical religious movement based on the teaching of Pythagoras that was undergoing a revival in the first century CE. These Pythagoreans would know the meaning of this strange number and it highlights the symbolic nature of John's gospel. The fish were caught on the occasion of Christ's third and last post-resurrection appearance to the disciples in John's gospel. The disciples en masse were referred to often as "the Twelve". If three and twelve are two sides of a right-angled triangle, Pythagoras's theorem teaches that the hypotenuse is three squared plus twelve squared, which is, you guessed it, one hundred and fifty-three! So embedded in the story of a seemingly miraculous catch of fish is a message about wholeness (3) and completion (12), God's purpose working out. Even more ingenious is the fact that the square root of 153 – the length of the hypotenuse of the triangle – is 12.37. This is the number of lunar months in a solar year, which would also have been well known by Pythagoreans, and may have indicated to them that the Jesus, who had performed the miracle, was identified with God, who created the universe. Clever stuff!

The more we dig into the gospel of John, the more we see the significance of numbers. Why was that? The gospel of John was addressed to a Greco-Roman audience steeped in astrology. Religion and mythology were often interpreted with reference to the planets, and a miracle worked with the numbers of the sky would symbolize resonance with the forces of the cosmos. As the Church later began purging itself of pagan symbolism, these meanings were lost.

There are more significant numbers in John. In chapter six, the author of John repeats the story told in Matthew, Mark, and Luke, which were written earlier, of Jesus feeding the five thousand (men only, plus many women and children) with two fishes and five loaves. At the end of the story, the remaining fragments fill twelve baskets. The numbers in this story, repeated in all four gospels, are two, five, and twelve – these are significant in the ancient world. Two is the number of the large celestial bodies, the sun and moon. Five is the number of planets visible to the naked eye. Twelve is the number of divisions in the heavens, the zodiac. Jesus created a miracle with the multitude, feeding more than five thousand on two fish and five loaves. In using those numbers, the author is indicating a correspondence between who Jesus was and who created the heavens. The pattern of Jesus' miracle, as symbolized by two, five, and twelve, is identical to the pattern of heaven. The numbers are the same, the difference is in scale. It is to show the link between Father and Son, for those who were aware of the significance of the numbers. The miracle of Creation is reproduced at an earthly scale by the Son – "Thy will be done, on earth as it is in Heaven." Link this with the 153 fish at the end of John, and we have another reference to the heavens. As already mentioned, the square root of one hundred and fifty-three, 12.37, is the number of lunar cycles in a solar year, and therefore symbolizes the relationship between the sun and moon as witnessed from the earth. This relationship, then as now, determines the cycles of day and night, the seasons, the weather, and the tides, all of which were understood in ancient culture.

Summary

Numbers mattered greatly to many of the biblical authors and were used to signify importance and connection, giving an underlying message in the stories that were told, particularly in the Gospel of John and Revelation. This is yet another reason for letting go of literalism and appreciating the ingenious construction of the writers of the Bible. The gospel writers were not writing down an eye-witness account as it was told to them. They were deliberately constructing stories that weaved together bits of oral tradition they knew of with justifications and "proof texts" they found in the Hebrew Scriptures, and deeper symbolic meanings that they could include. In doing so, they often used numbers as part of the symbolism. Their crafted tales were then released for us to make of them what we can. The Church teaching which developed has for the most part accepted these mythological tales as literal, rather than a balance of actual happenings laced with human creativity and ingenuity. Keeping a watch for the symbolism of numbers can be an indicator to the discerning reader that the author has created some inventive underlying indicators.

Questions for Reflection

1. Have you noticed the significance of numbers in the Bible before? Have you heard any teaching in church?
2. Do you have favourite numbers? If so, reflect on what it is about them that attracts you.
3. Look up the Fibonacci Series and the Golden Ratio, then reflect on why that particular ratio should be aesthetically appealing. Is there a built-in beauty to the universe? (See www.investopedia.com/articles/technical/04/033104.asp)

Further Resources

https://en.wikipedia.org/wiki/Biblical_numerology
https://www.churchtimes.co.uk/articles/2019/26-april/faith/faith-features/divine-numerology
https://crossexamined.org/reference-guide-biblical-numerology/

Epilogue and Explanation

This is the second book in what I have termed "The Wisdom Series", in which I am seeking to begin reframing Christianity for the twenty-first century. The frame in which I now understand it is that of a much greater cosmology with an ancient lineage, that of "Wisdom". This embraces the universe of three dimensions as we know it, but places that within a much greater context of subtle realms of finer energies and planes of being, that some call the "imaginal realm". This teaching details a level of existence beyond our physical universe, beyond the laws of nature as we currently understand them, beyond what we can see, hear and touch. Christianity has always referred to this realm, as have other faith traditions, but its frame of reference has been very limited and basic in its understanding, apart from those mystics and seers who have entered consciously into these other realms and then imparted some of that wisdom to others.

In the Perennial Wisdom teachings, the divine essence or spirit of each human being works through a soul which is sheathed in materiality, called the personality, consisting of mind, emotions and physical body. The soul is eternal and is reincarnated many times into a new personality over eons of time, as it gains in understanding of the meaning of being conscious. In so doing, it progresses through different stages, or initiations, until it reaches a stage where it no longer needs to return to earthly physical existence but can go on to further and higher states of being. Some humans have already reached that stage and have gone before us. They are the "cloud of witnesses" referred to in Hebrews 12:1 and from this exalted dimension some Great Ones choose to return to serve humanity. Jesus was such a one, a forerunner, and is the "pioneer and perfecter of our faith" (Hebrews 12:2), i.e. the trailblazer, the path-maker, the one who came to serve and has now gone before us to show us the way and aid us on the path of transformation. In doing so, he changed something for all humanity, and in this sense he "saved" us. (There will be more on this in the next book in this series.)

* * *

This is just a tiny scratch on the surface of the Perennial Wisdom philosophy. It's not a religion, as all religions can fit into its framework. Its long lineage is indicated in many writings, particularly from the Enlightenment onwards, but stretching right back to the early mystery schools of Greek and Egyptian origins. In more recent times, it has been enlarged and expanded upon in the writings of authors such as Helena Blavatsky, Annie Besant, Charles Leadbeater, Alice Bailey, Roberto Assagioli, Vera Stanley, Dane Rudhyar, Aldous Huxley, Michael Robbins, William Meader, and in a more popular form, the *Conversations with God* books by Neale Donald Walsch. Some of these various sources are termed "channelled" writings, which simply means divinely inspired writings from a higher source, much as the biblical texts are considered to be. While these authors mentioned may be considered to be "outside" the Christian framework, there are many within Christianity who are currently writing and teaching aspects of the Perennial Wisdom, such as Fr. Richard Rohr, Revd Dr. Cynthia Bourgeault, Ilia Delio, Judy Cannato and Revd Matthew Fox, building on the work of earlier contemplatives and mystics such as Pierre Teilhard de Chardin, Bede Griffiths, Thomas Merton, Thomas Keating, and Raimon Pannikar, who is quoted as saying "I left Europe [for India] as a Christian, I discovered I was a Hindu and returned as a Buddhist without ever having ceased to be a Christian." There is also a whole raft of poets, artists and philosophers who draw their inspiration from forms of this teaching.

The whole Wisdom cosmology encompasses and speaks into

everything that happens in the physical realm and particularly all areas of human endeavour – religion, economics, politics, education, health, relationships, psychology, etc. To get into the detail is something beyond this book, but to give an idea of its purpose, it seeks to encourage the following laws and principles:

- **Right Human Relationships** – Foundational is the need for loving understanding and compassion, non-judgmentalism, and acceptance of the inherent dignity of every human being. It is a commitment to finding wise outcomes in all relationships.

- **Goodwill**, which is a powerful principle, an attitude of being towards all other beings, human and non-human, wanting the best for them. It is a quality that generates kindness and warmth. It is the will-to-good.

- Unanimity, which is a form of group consciousness, appreciating the need to work together positively for a better world. It puts agreement and union of the Whole above the individual. The consensus so achieved is inclusive and transformative.

- **Group Endeavour** – seeking cooperation and collaboration rather than competition and antagonism. It is the creative working together whereby use is made of mutual qualities. The ability to work with a common team purpose demonstrates the co-operation and interdependence of all.

- Spiritual Approach is the gradual path of transformation. It begins when we start to turn our attention from the material world around us and begin searching for a relationship with our inner true essence, our Higher Self, our Soul. Personal wisdom is acquired daily through all relationships and experiences when they are viewed in the light of the Soul.

- Essential Divinity is the recognition of the vital essence at our very core that colours all our relationships revealing that we are all different and yet all the same, coming from the One Life, the Divine Source.

Within this open and expansive framework, Christianity and most other faiths can be expressed. Every religious tradition has its own scriptures to which it holds dear, yet this wisdom stream runs through all of them, expressed in the culture and context of the particular faith. In this rapidly changing world, a larger container is urgently need to overcome the seeming disparities and enmities between the different religious factions, and to encompass the huge rise of alternative and complementary spiritual, psychological and therapeutic practices which have emerged in recent years. The Perennial Wisdom teachings are enormous in their remit and give a presentation of a spiritual cosmology and psychology which is based in the existence of subtle energy realms and different spiritual planes constituting the makeup of the human being and all material reality.

In a simple analogy, it can be likened to a car which takes you from A to B safely. The purpose of the car is for transport to a different place. Most do not need to know the workings of the engine and its science, only that we can rely upon them. Some do need to look into the engineering, the chemistry and physics and subtle details of how a car works. Like a car, the wisdom philosophy has a whole host of levels of understanding from which to access it and understand it, but not everyone needs to be a mechanic or an electrical engineer or a research scientist.

* * *

New concepts are always a challenge to traditional ways of thinking. The next book in this wisdom series will meet one of the biggest challenges head on, the nature of Christ Jesus. The Nicene Creed puts it like this:

We believe in one Lord Jesus Christ, the only begotten Son of God, begotten of the Father before all the world. Light of Light, very God of very God, begotten, not made: who for us men and for our salvation came down from heaven and was incarnate by the Holy Spirit of the Virgin Mary, and was made man.

But is there a distinction to be made between Jesus and the Christ? What would that distinction be? How can we reinterpret Christianity in the light of an expanded view of Jesus of Nazareth and the Christ? The next edition in this series will delve deeply into this puzzle.

Author Biography

Revd Don MacGregor, B.Sc. M.A., is a retired Anglican priest living in St Davids, Wales. He was a science teacher for 13 years before ordination, and his Christian journey has moved from evangelical and charismatic to mystical and esoteric with aspects of contemporary holistic spirituality, and an emphasis on meditation and contemplative prayer. He is passionate to find a new way forward for Christianity which incorporates twenty-first-century science and worldviews. He is also an active member of the World Community for Christian Meditation, CANA (Christians Awakening to New Awareness) and the Progressive Christian Network.

Previous titles

MacGregor, Don, 2012. *Blue Sky God: The Evolution of Science and Christianity.* Alresford UK: Circle Books, John Hunt Publishing

Blue Sky God interprets some new scientific theories with blue sky thinking to bring radical insights into God, Jesus and humanity, drawing also on some deep wells from the past in the writings of the early Christians. In an accessible style, it looks at science research and theories in areas such as quantum physics and consciousness, epigenetics, morphic resonance and the zero-point field. From there, seeing God as the compassionate consciousness at the ground of being, it draws together strands to do with unitive consciousness and the Wisdom way of the heart. Throughout, it seeks to encourage an evolution in understanding of the Christian message by reinterpreting much of the theological language and meaning that has become "orthodoxy" in the West. In doing so, it challenges many of the standard assumptions of Western Christianity. It outlines a spiritual path that includes elements in all the world's great religions, is not exclusive, and yet has a place of centrality for Jesus the Christ as a Wisdom teacher of the path of transformative love.

Endorsements

This is a brave and important book, dispelling confusions and misunderstandings, and making clear the relevance of a Christian path today. MacGregor integrates modern science, mystical experience, history, philosophy and biblical scholarship in a new synthesis that shows how religious practice is evolving in the twenty-first century. I particularly enjoyed his discussions of the Holy Trinity and the Virgin Birth. As the old dogmas of science and materialism break down, he gives good grounds for hope.
Dr. Rupert Sheldrake, author of *The Science Delusion* and *A New Science of Life*

This is a fascinating and profound exploration of the deep resonances between the discoveries of the Christian Mystics and those of modern science. We are living in an era in which mystical and scientific proof are coming ever closer to open up for the human race a wholly new way of approaching reality and potentially solving the enormous problems that keeping science and religion apart have created. I salute the courage of this book and hope it will attain a large and enthusiastic audience.
Andrew Harvey, author of *The Hope: a Guide to Sacred Activism, Son of Man* and others

Blue Sky God is a passionate and inspiring call for us to understand the true message and example of Jesus in the contemporary world. With careful scholarship and flowing prose, Don MacGregor explains the insights of modern science and spirituality, and how they provide a new context for the healing and redemptive heart of Christian spirituality. With today's current interest in eastern and indigenous religions, it is important that we also appreciate and bring home the true power and love of Jesus. Don

MacGregor succeeds in this significant task. The Appendix with its reformulations of the Christian Healing Service and Holy Communion also make *Blue Sky God* a valuable asset. I warmly recommend this book.

William Bloom, author of *The Power of Modern Spirituality*

MacGregor, Don, 2020. *Christianity Expanding: Into Universal Spirituality.* **Alresford UK: Christian Alternative Books, John Hunt Publishing**

Christianity Expanding: Into Universal Spirituality takes us on a whistle-stop tour of the areas that need updating if Christianity is to flourish in the twenty-first century. New science, ecological concern and the need for new theology are all converging into a maelstrom of change. With broad brushstrokes on a big canvas, a path of personal transformation is charted, drawing on the mysterious Perennial Wisdom teachings that have survived down the ages. Pulling no punches, Don MacGregor delves into typically taboo subjects such as reincarnation, drawing a distinction between Jesus and the Christ. This dynamic first volume of "The Wisdom Series" is an initial outline of areas that demand ongoing exploration.

Endorsements

Christianity is evolving rapidly today. Don MacGregor's book is a lucid and thoughtful guide to this process, and shows how the essential core teachings of Christianity can be disentangled from unhelpful interpretations that stand in the way of a living Christian faith in the twenty-first century.

Dr Rupert Sheldrake, author of *A New Science of Life* and *The Science Delusion*

With his deep and extensive understanding of Christianity and Perennial Wisdom teachings, Don MacGregor shares in this lucid, profound and wonderfully compassionate book that they, and indeed all major spiritual traditions, are; "the path of the evolution of human consciousness". Vitally, *Christianity Expanding* gifts its readers with a revitalisation of Jesus' call to love one another and affirms that we have now reached the stage in our collective evolution when we can begin to do so on a global level.

Dr Jude Currivan, cosmologist, author of *The Cosmic Hologram* and co-founder of *WholeWorld-View*

This is a really helpful and stimulating book for anyone interested in the future of the Church and Christianity. Concise, easy to read and full of helpful insights it combines a classical understanding of theology with all the new awarenesses of a contemporary holistic approach. If I had a magic wand, every clergyperson would read *Christianity Expanding*, as well as every pagan and witch with space in their heart for the Christian message.

William Bloom, author of *The Power of Modern Spirituality* and *The Endorphin Effect*

Note to Reader

Thank you for purchasing *Expanding Scriptures: Lost and Found.* My sincere hope is that you derived as much from reading this book as I have in creating it. If you have a few moments, please feel free to add your review of the book at your favourite online site for feedback. Also, if you would like to connect with other books that I have coming in the near future, please visit my website for news on upcoming works, to sign up for new blog posts.

https://www.donmacgregor.co.uk

Don MacGregor, donmacg@live.co.uk

Appendix 1

The Old Testament in a nutshell

In my evangelical charismatic days, I was coached in the Bible by a dear friend who encouraged me to learn a programme of Bible verses, and also to read through the good book in a year's worth of daily readings. I did that, and was very grateful for it. I got a picture of the broad sweep of scripture, and in later years I put that to good use in a sermon in which I tried to capture the story of the Old Testament. Here it is.

(**Note:** as this is a sermon given in 2012, I have left in place the original term *Old Testament* rather than *the Hebrew Scriptures*.)

In the beginning, back in the mists and myths of time, there was God, who created. God created light, and from that light came everything else. I don't picture God as an old man with a beard, I see God as the ground of being, more like the cosmic consciousness from which everything emerged. A good nine billion years later, the earth formed, and a few billion years after that, Homo sapiens came along. This all happened in the first six "days" of creation.

After this creation, during which we are told that "God saw that it was good", we find a theme in which humanity kept *getting it wrong*. We first hear of Adam and Eve, who *got it wrong*. They listened to the wrong advice from the serpent and were sent out of the Garden of Eden on their own. They had two sons Cain and Abel, the two brothers who didn't get on. They *got it very wrong* – Cain killed Abel. Cain was cast out of the family.

So Adam and Eve had another son Seth. From Seth, there were many others, who all lived a very long time – Methuselah was the longest at 969 years – and then there was Noah, who built an ark because everyone else *got it wrong*, but not him – humankind had become wicked and evil. God sorted it out with the flood. And so God started again with Noah, Shem, Ham and

Japheth – and their nameless wives! (Noah was a mere 500 years old when they were born.) Then another long time passed. It is obviously a mythological story up to this point – it conveys truth but is not to be taken literally.

Abraham

The Hebrew lineage begins properly with Abraham (about 1900 BCE). Abraham (first known as Abram) came from Haran, a place thought to be in Turkey, near the border with Syria. God said that Abraham would be the father of "many nations" and that Abraham and his descendants should circumcise the male babies on the eighth day after birth to seal the contract. Following God's instructions, he travelled to Canaan.

From Abraham came Isaac, then Jacob (whose name was changed to Israel), who had twelve sons, giving rise to the twelve "tribes" of Israel. One of Jacob's sons, Joseph, was sold into slavery by his bothers, who *got it wrong,* and was taken to Egypt. Eventually, because Joseph could interpret dreams, he rose through the ranks to become the Pharaoh's right-hand man. That led to Jacob and his family coming to Egypt during a great famine and later their many descendants become slaves in Egypt (we don't know how, but presumably they *got it wrong*). And the Israelites suffered through the harsh treatment of the Pharaoh. Along came Moses, the baby in the rush basket, brought up in the royal court, who also *got it wrong* and killed an Egyptian and was cast out of Egypt for forty years. Then came his godly call at the burning bush to free the Israelites, followed by the plagues. Moses led the Exodus of the Israelites from Egypt, freeing them from bondage and the Covenant of God with the Hebrew nation was made in the Passover of the Angel of death.

It took them forty years of wandering in the wilderness and a lot of soul-searching to get to Canaan, the promised land. On the way, at Mount Sinai, God gave the Ten Commandments for the people of Israel to obey in order that He was to be their God.

There were constant problems with the Jewish people believing in idols and other "gods". They kept *getting it wrong.*

The Promised Land

Finally the people reached the Promised Land and settled there after Moses' death. Canaan was divided up into areas for the twelve tribes, named after the twelve sons of Jacob, or Israel as he was renamed. So the twelve areas of the nation of Israel were established, mostly through the warring leadership of Joshua. They appointed "Judges" who led the people until about 1000 BCE. But the people wanted a king, and the last Judge, Samuel, anointed Saul as king – until Saul *got it wrong.* Samuel then anointed David as king. David was a warrior king and subdued the surrounding tribes, the Canaanites, Hittites, Philistines, Phoenicians, Moabites, Ammonites, etc. King David and his son King Solomon then led a united, strong country. Solomon's Israel was big – but after Solomon's death, it all fell apart in family disputes. They *got it wrong again.* And so the divided kingdom was formed.

Northern Kingdom – still called Israel, consisted of 10 "tribes"; this group included what eventually became Samaria.

Southern Kingdom – called Judah, though consisting of both the "tribes" of Judah and Benjamin; this group included the city of Jerusalem.

The Northern Kingdom fell to the Assyrians around 722 BCE. The Assyrians moved the leaders to other places in their empire, never to return. Those that were left intermarried and became of mixed race. Hence the Samaritans were detested by the Judeans when it came to the New Testament times.

The Southern Kingdom fell to the Babylonians in 586 BCE. All the leaders of the nation were taken off to Babylon, and were in exile there for seventy years. It is thought that this is when the first five books of the Old Testament were written down, to remind the Israelites of where they had come from, and to give them hope in the God who had given them the promised land. Then along came the Persians, who were much more lenient, and repatriated all those who had been taken from their homeland by the Babylonians. Nehemiah and Ezra led the Israelites from their seventy-year exile in Babylon, back to Israel to rebuild the temple. Although the Hebrews rebuilt the Temple in Jerusalem in 515 BCE, they never regained strength and were conquered by the Greek empire of Alexander the Great, and eventually by the Romans.

The Hebrew people explained their struggles with the Assyrians and the Babylonians and their exile from their country in terms of their disobedience to God. They kept *getting it wrong*. They kept going back to a belief in idols and heathen "gods" (mostly resulting from their marrying non-Jews who brought in outside religions). The prophets, people like Elijah, Elisha, Isaiah, Jeremiah, Ezekiel were spokesmen for God to the people and to their leaders. They often disagreed with the men in power and had no fear of expressing their messages from God – generally directing against the idolatry and "false gods". All this was written about in the various books at the beginning of the Old Testament. Then comes all the rest, a mixture of story, sayings, poetry, songs and prophecy.

In the later prophetic writings, there was a general belief that they would be rescued by a *Messiah* who would lead them back to being their own nation again, and that the "Day of the Lord" would come, when all things come to a conclusion. Which, of course, leads us up to the New Testament and the time of Jesus the Messiah.

So there we are, the Old Testament in a nutshell, about as condensed as you can get. They are more often called the Hebrew Scriptures these days, the story of the Hebrew people, their beliefs, their struggles and their growing understanding that the God they followed was not just the God of their tribe, not just the God of their region, but the only God, the one God, whose name, as was revealed to Moses, as "I am that I am", Yahweh, I am Being. This is the God of life, the One God, in whom we live and move and have our being.

Bibliography

Armstrong, Karen, 2008. *The Bible: The Biography.* London: Atlantic Books

Baumann, Lynn C., Baumann Ward J., Bourgeault, Cynthia, 2008. *The Luminous Gospels: Thomas, Mary Magdalene and Philip.* Texas: Praxis Publishing

Bladon, Lee, 2007. *The Science of Spirituality-Integrating Science, Psychology, Philosophy, Spirituality & Religion.* Esotericscience. org

Borg, Marcus, Wright N.T., 1999. *The Meaning of Jesus: Two Visions.* London: SPCK

Borg, Marcus, 2003. *The Heart of Christianity: Rediscovering a Life of Faith.* San Francisco CA: HarperSanFrancisco

Borg, Marcus, 2011. *Speaking Christian: Recovering the Lost Meaning of Christian Words.* London: SPCK

Bourgeault, Cynthia, 2010. *The Meaning of Mary Magdalene: Discovering the Woman at the Heart of Christianity.* Boston MA: Shambhala Publications

Cannato, Judy, 2010. *Field of Compassion: How the New Cosmology is Transforming Spiritual Life.* Notre Dame IN: Sorin Books

Davies Stevan, 2002. *The Gospel of Thomas: Annotated and Explained.* London: Darton, Longman & Todd

Delio, Ilia, 2013. *The Unbearable Wholeness of Being: God, Evolution and the Power of Love.* New York: Orbis Books

De Quillan, Jehanne, 2011. *The Gospel of the Beloved Companion: The Complete Gospel of Mary Magdalene.* North Charleston CA: Create Space

Ehrman, Bart D., 2003. *Lost Christianities: The Battles for Scripture and the Faith We Never Knew.* New York: Oxford University Press

Ehrman, Bart D., 2005. *Misquoting Jesus: The Story Behind Who Changed the Bible and Why.* New York HarperCollins

Grant, Robert & Freedman, David, 1993. *The Secret Sayings of Jesus.* New York: Barnes & Noble

Hodson, Geoffrey, 1993. *Hidden Wisdom in the Holy Bible, Vol. 1.* Wheaton IL: Quest Books

Henson, J., 2004. *Good as New: A Radical Retelling of the Scriptures.* Winchester UK: O Books

Henson, J., 2010. *Wide Awake Worship: Hymns and Prayers Renewed for the 21st Century.* Winchester UK: O Books

Holloway, Richard, 2001. *Doubts and Loves: What is Left of Christianity.* Edinburgh: Canongate Books

Johnson, Luke T, 1986. *The Writings of the New Testament: An Interpretation.* London: Fortress Press

Laird, M., 2006. *Into the Silent Land – A Guide to the Christian Practice of Meditation.* Oxford: Oxford University Press

Lester, Meera, 2006. *The Everything Mary Magdalene Book: the life and legacy of Jesus' most misunderstood disciple.* Avon MA: Adams Media

MacGregor, Don, 2012. *Blue Sky God: The Evolution of Science and Christianity.* Alresford UK: Circle Books, John Hunt Publishing

MacGregor, Don, 2020. *Christianity Expanding: Into Universal Spirituality.* Alresford UK: Christian Alternative Books, John Hunt Publishing

Meyer, Marvin, 2004. *The Gospels of Mary: The Secret Tradition of Mary Magdalene the Companion of Jesus.* New York: HarperCollins

Meyer, Marvin (ed.), 2007. *The Nag Hammadi Scriptures: The International Edition.* New York: HarperCollins

Pagels, Elaine, 2004. *Beyond Belief: The Secret Gospel of Thomas.* London: Pan MacMillan

Pagels, Elaine & King, Karen, 2007. *Reading Judas: The Gospel of Judas and the Shaping of Christianity.* London: Penguin Books

Rohr, Richard, 2008. *Things Hidden: Scripture as Spirituality.* Cincinnati OH: St Anthony Messenger Press

Spong, John Shelby, 1996. *Liberating the Gospels: Reading the Bible with Jewish Eyes.* San Francisco CA: HarperSanFrancisco

Taussig, Hal (ed.), 2015. *A New New Testament: A Bible for the 21st Century.* New York: Houghton Mifflin Harcourt Publishing Co

Winterhalter, Robert, 1988, *The Fifth Gospel: A Verse-by-verse New Age Commentary on the Gospel of Thomas.* San Francisco: Harper & Row

THE NEW OPEN SPACES

Throughout the two thousand years of Christian tradition there
have been, and still are, groups and individuals that exist in
the margins and upon the edge of faith. But in Christianity's
contrapuntal history it has often been these outcasts and
pioneers that have forged contemporary orthodoxy out
of former radicalism as belief evolves to engage with and
encompass the ever-changing social and scientific realities. Real
faith lies not in the comfortable certainties of the Orthodox,
but somewhere in a half-glimpsed hinterland on the dirt track
to Emmaus, where the Death of God meets the Resurrection,
where the supernatural Christ meets the historical Jesus,
and where the revolution liberates both the oppressed and
the oppressors.

Welcome to Christian Alternative... a space at the edge where
the light shines through.
If you have enjoyed this book, why not tell other readers by
posting a review on your preferred book site.

Recent bestsellers from Christian Alternative are:

Bread Not Stones
The Autobiography of An Eventful Life
Una Kroll
The spiritual autobiography of a truly remarkable woman
and a history of the struggle for ordination in the Church of
England.
Paperback: 978-1-78279-804-0 ebook: 978-1-78279-805-7

The Quaker Way
A Rediscovery
Rex Ambler
Although fairly well known, Quakerism is not well understood.
The purpose of this book is to explain how Quakerism works as
a spiritual practice.
Paperback: 978-1-78099-657-8 ebook: 978-1-78099-658-5

Blue Sky God
The Evolution of Science and Christianity
Don MacGregor
Quantum consciousness, morphic fields and blue-sky
thinking about God and Jesus the Christ.
Paperback: 978-1-84694-937-1 ebook: 978-1-84694-938-8

Celtic Wheel of the Year
Tess Ward
An original and inspiring selection of prayers combining
Christian and Celtic Pagan traditions, and interweaving their
calendars into a single pattern of prayer for every morning
and night of the year.
Paperback: 978-1-90504-795-6

Christian Atheist
Belonging without Believing
Brian Mountford
Christian Atheists don't believe in God but miss him: especially
the transcendent beauty of his music, language, ethics, and
community.
Paperback: 978-1-84694-439-0 ebook: 978-1-84694-929-6

Compassion Or Apocalypse?
A Comprehensible Guide to the Thoughts of René Girard
James Warren
How René Girard changes the way we think about God and the
Bible, and its relevance for our apocalypse-threatened world.
Paperback: 978-1-78279-073-0 ebook: 978-1-78279-072-3

Diary Of A Gay Priest
The Tightrope Walker
Rev. Dr. Malcolm Johnson
Full of anecdotes and amusing stories, but the Church is still a
dangerous place for a gay priest.
Paperback: 978-1-78279-002-0 ebook: 978-1-78099-999-9

Do You Need God?
Exploring Different Paths to Spirituality Even For Atheists
Rory J.Q. Barnes
An unbiased guide to the building blocks of spiritual belief.
Paperback: 978-1-78279-380-9 ebook: 978-1-78279-379-3

Readers of ebooks can buy or view any of these bestsellers by clicking on the live link in the title. Most titles are published in paperback and as an ebook. Paperbacks are available in traditional bookshops. Both print and ebook formats are available online.

Find more titles and sign up to our readers' newsletter at
http://www.johnhuntpublishing.com/christianity
Follow us on Facebook at
https://www.facebook.com/ChristianAlternative